To my friend Stella Henshaw

with best
wishes —

Harold Marsh.
Feb 19 1968

GIVE US THE TOOLS

Also by Henry Viscardi, Jr.

A MAN'S STATURE: The story of
Hank Viscardi and J.O.B.

GIVE US THE TOOLS

by

HENRY VISCARDI, JR.

Introduction by ELEANOR ROOSEVELT

PAUL S. ERIKSSON, INC.
NEW YORK

First Printing, 1959

Second Printing, 1963

Third Printing, 1966

Library of Congress Catalog Card Number: 59-10005

Manufactured in the United States of America by The Haddon Craftsmen, Inc., Scranton, Pa.

To my mother

PUBLISHERS' FOREWORD

The story of Henry Viscardi, Jr. is a story of courage, dedication and perseverance.

It begins May 10, 1912, in New York City where he was born, the son of an immigrant Italian barber. Only it wasn't quite that routine, for young Henry was born with only two short stumps where legs should have been. He spent the first seven years of his life in hospitals while doctors performed operation after operation. He came to know his nurses better than his parents.

At the end of seven years, he was allowed to go home, his stumps encased in heavy padded boots that looked like boxing gloves. Then, instead of the warmth and understanding he had become accustomed to, he discovered an awesome world of staring, over-sympathetic and well-meaning adults, and the thoughtless cruelty of taunting playmates. Somehow he learned to live with both, laughing off the taunts, growing immune to the stares, rejecting the pity.

It is to his mother, however, that Henry Viscardi gives most of the credit for nurturing and cultivating a healthy attitude toward the world, notwithstanding. From her deep sense of humanity and simple wisdom, the boy drew comfort, protection, maturity, and that infinitely valuable quality, acceptance.

With the cries of "ape man" ringing in his ears, young

Viscardi went through elementary school and high school in eight years. At Fordham University he paid his own way by refereeing basketball games, waiting on tables and covering school sports for the *New York Times*. After three years, he left to take a job as a law clerk and attend St. John's Law School at night. Soon he became a tax expert for the government, working hard, rising rapidly.

One day about this time "Hank" learned from his doctor that his stumps were wearing out, that he might soon lose his mobility. Unless something "impossible" could be done, Henry Viscardi would have to spend the rest of his life in a wheelchair. Happily, something could be done.

Dr. Robert R. Yanover, Hank's doctor, told him there was a chance, a long shot but nevertheless a chance, that artificial legs could be made for him. It was almost too much to hope for . . .

On a momentous day a few months later, Henry Viscardi, Jr., 26, born legless and matured at three feet eight inches high, put on his first pair of long pants, stood up erect, looked in a mirror and saw a new man. He saw a man five feet, eight inches tall who no longer wore boxing glove boots.

Dr. Yanover refused payment for his work. "But someday," he said, "do something to help other cripples. Then our account will be squared."

As World War II began, Hank tried in vain to enlist.

Accepted by the Red Cross as field officer, he was assigned to Walter Reed Hospital in Washington, D.C. There he worked closely with amputees, teaching them to walk, giving them hope, confidence and courage. It was here he first met the world-famous rehabilitation specialist, Dr. Howard A. Rusk.

After the war, Hank worked for the Mutual Broadcasting System as "leg-man" for the sports department. Soon he moved to Burlington Mills as Personnel Director. Married now, father of two daughters, he and his wife Lucile owned their own home in Kings Point, Long Island—a house they built themselves. Henry Viscardi, Jr. was a fast-rising young executive with a bright future in the business world, a world apart from the disabled.

But the fame he had gained with the Red Cross as a rehabilitation expert tracked him down. The year was 1949. His old friend, Dr. Rusk, prevailed upon him to join him and others in a venture called "Just One Break" (J.O.B.), an organization being formed to help place disabled men and women, many of them forgotten war veterans, in gainful employment. Urged by his wife to accept, Hank yielded, giving up his prosperous job to become a pioneer in the field of rehabilitation.

From J.O.B. it was a short hop to the vacant garage in Hempstead, Long Island, where Viscardi founded Abilities, Inc., with $8000 in borrowed funds in 1952. Through hard work, resourcefulness and a never-say-die attitude, the company grew. And as Abilities has grown since, so have the opportunities for disabled men and women throughout the world.

Today Henry Viscardi, Jr. is president of this thriving company. *Give Us the Tools* is his story and the story of these amazing people.

PREFACE

I have wished for some time to share intimately some of the mixed experiences I have known in this unique enterprise. Living and working closely with a company made up of disabled people have had their moments of inspiration, as well as their moments of tears and laughter. These I would like to share with many.

Once, while speaking in Washington, D.C., I was severely challenged from the audience for referring to the people at Abilities as "my people." I had not, as my critic inferred, pretended to own them. They are "my people" only because I have felt so much a part of those for whom and with whom I serve, for I, as they, have known many years of crippling disillusionment, the ridicule, the rejection, which comes from being different, not the same, as others.

On lecture platforms and in articles during the past years, I have told only parts of this story. Now I have the opportunity to tell all of it—the story of these extraordinary people in search of ordinary destinies.

For their contribution to this book, there are many people to whom grateful acknowledgment should be made. Obviously such a daring attempt, beginning only as an unprecedented idea and growing because of the strength of its disabled workers, must have had many friends or it could not have been possible, nor could it have survived. I am, therefore, deeply indebted to so very many.

To Lynn and George Groh I am most grateful for editorial assistance. Their enthusiasm for the work was an inspiration to me in the preparation of the manuscript.

I am grateful to Paul Eriksson and Richard Taplinger who have believed in this book and have been so very helpful in making it possible.

I wish to acknowledge the research efforts of Helen Buckler, of Arthur Nierenberg, Ellen Vaughan, Louis Blersch, Florence Fiedelman, and my associates at Abilities, Inc.

But I want to acknowledge the special debt I owe to Garrison Siskin and my friends in industry, commerce, labor, medicine and government, who have contributed their faith and energies to this great ideal. Without them there could have been no Abilities, Inc. To Mary E. Switzer, to Dr. Howard A. Rusk, to Bernard M. Baruch, to the Members of our Board of Directors, to my colleagues in industry and labor who have helped make all this possible, I am also deeply indebted.

Above all, I wish to acknowledge the debt I owe the workers at Abilities, Inc. To their wives and families who have believed in them as they have believed in the possibility of fulfilling our dream, I am truly grateful.

If this book brings comfort to some other disabled person who seeks the dignity of a productive life, I shall be thankful. If it serves to inspire another community to follow this example by establishing a similar company, I and all those who have worked for such a success shall be more than amply rewarded.

In fact, if it should change the life of but one disabled person from dependence on the charity of community or family to fullness and richness, with the dignity of self-sufficiency, then I shall be richly rewarded. For this was, after all, the goal we set when Abilities, Inc. was founded.

HENRY VISCARDI, JR.

CONTENTS

INTRODUCTION

by

Eleanor Roosevelt

Seven years ago Henry Viscardi wrote a book called *A Man's Stature*. This book was largely the author's personal story of courage and determination in his own rehabilitation. But it also told the story of the unique and highly successful Just One Break Committee (J.O.B.) formed to help others with physical disabilities secure employment. I knew both of those stories before they were written, for I have known Henry Viscardi since World War II, when he began his work with disabled servicemen.

When Henry wrote his first book, he was forty years old and had at that age fulfilled sufficient ambitions to satisfy most young men. He and his lovely wife Lucile had three (now four) delightful young daughters and he was the Executive Director of Just One Break, Inc. He had the satisfaction of both personal success and helping thousands of others with physical disabilities bring their dreams to fulfillment through finding the dignity which comes only through useful, gainful work. J.O.B. also had made a significant contribution to the changing of attitudes of employers toward hiring the handicapped and had established a pattern which many other communities, both here and abroad, had followed in developing their own voluntary placement services for the handicapped.

But Henry Viscardi was not satisfied. There were some who came to Just One Break seeking help to whom the doors of opportunity and employment were closed because of the severity of their disabilities. Henry Viscardi was convinced in his heart that these persons, too, could be useful, productive workers if they only could have an opportunity. So he set about creating that opportunity. With four others, he decided to start a new type of venture—not the traditional sheltered workshop in which the handicapped so frequently work at menial tasks and at low wages in a sub-standard environment. He was determined this should be a laboratory of human engineering where severely disabled people could prove by their own efforts that they could successfully perform complex tasks in a competitive industrial setting.

They called their company "Abilities, Inc." for they had confidence that their abilities far outweighed their disabilities. There were four employees when they set up for business in an old garage. Two of these employees were in wheelchairs. Among the four, there were but five usable arms and one usable leg.

This book, *Give Us the Tools,* is the story of Abilities, Inc., of what has been achieved in but seven short years. I had also known of this story before it was written for I watched this dream come to fruition.

In my travels throughout the United States and in many other nations, I have been concerned with many things, but the underlying factor which is basic to all these concerns is human rights. Human rights and all that this phrase implies is based on the value of human worth and of personal dignity. The story of Abilities, Inc., of its employees and of its friends, are each individual stories of personal dignity and human rights, which have an influence far beyond the working and personal lives of its employees. They are stories which personify and symbolize the human rights and personal dignity which we in the United States strive to achieve for all of our citizens.

GIVE US THE TOOLS

CHAPTER ONE

LONG JOURNEY ON SHORT LEGS

A blind man could see it. He could stand in the middle of the big shop floor at Abilities, Inc., and know at once what it was all about.

He would hear the tap of canes and crutches, the rubber-tired sounds of wheelchairs passing up and down the aisles. The sounds made by afflicted people.

He'd hear others things, too. Machines whirring. Hammers striking metal. Sounds of people working.

Yes, a blind man could see it easily enough. It would not surprise him to find afflicted people hard at work.

Unfortunately, there are those not blind who cannot see it. They are good people mostly, but they do not understand. They heap pity on the disabled, and smother them in a soft blanket of charity, and turn away in embarrassed shock from the crippled man who wants a job. They do not know that they are killing with kindness.

That's why Abilities exists. To prove that the disabled can help themselves if people everywhere will only give them a chance.

Abilities, Inc., is a factory run by and for the disabled. It was started in 1952 with one paralyzed worker in a grimy, unfurnished garage. Within five years it had grown to a million dollar business with more than three hundred employees in a shining new plant of its own. Behind every employee is the thrilling story of a human life rebuilt from ruins. Today, Abilities stands as a national and international model for all the world to see.

One of its executives, a man named Ray Leizer, wears two steel hooks in place of hands. If you ask him how he manages he'll observe drily that he's no handshaker, or backslapper, but he knows how to get things done.

A foreman in the packaging department was born without arms or legs. He has developed amazing ability to use his vestigial stumps. A woman who is both blind and deaf has served with sure-fingered skill on the production line. Another employee is so badly injured that he can neither sit nor stand. He reclines at his desk at a 45° angle, in a special sling of his own devising, and is one of the most valuable men in the plant. He works with his head and his wonderful hands.

Still another man lies on a litter, flat on his back,

and does a day's work every day. He has never thought of himself as a symbol but call him that if you like. He's down, but far from out.

The examples are endless. They can be summed up, perhaps, in the story of Jim Chapin. Five years ago a tumor on the spine left Jim paralyzed from the waist down. When they lifted him from the operating table the doctors said he would live—but he was finished for anything else. He was doomed to be a helpless hulk of a man for the rest of his days.

The doctors were wrong. At 62, confined to his wheelchair, Jim came to Abilities to start life over. He is 68 now, and still paralyzed, and holds an active, demanding job as a foreman in the mechanical assembly department. When asked recently about his plans for retirement, he reacted with an astonished grin.

"Retire?" he said. "Me? I think I'd go nuts!"

Abilities people feel that way about their jobs. Having lost the chance to work, and having found it again, they know what it is worth. They have a fierce pride in their hard-earned skills, a fierce determination not to be dependent and helpless ever again.

I am president of Abilities and I share this pride. Often I thank God that my own struggle with disability led me finally to take part in the Abilities adventure.

I learned about disability very early in life. I was born with twisted, malformed stumps where legs ought to be.

For the first six years of my life, the hospital was my home. Afterward I padded around the streets of New York on grotesque, cork-stuffed orthopedic boots. So short were my legs that my dangling arms almost touched the ground. Some of the boys in my block called me "ape man," and so I learned how to fight. I never did learn how to cope with that other insult, the condescending pat on the head.

When I was 25, I was only three feet eight inches tall. Then the miracle happened. A wonderful doctor named Robert Yanover took me to a crusty, brilliant old craftsman named George Dorsch, and between them they stood me up on ingenious aluminum legs. Suddenly I was five foot eight, and everyone recognized what I had known all along. I was a man.

Doc Yanover wouldn't take pay for what he had done. Or, rather, he wouldn't take any money. "Hank," he said, "maybe someday you'll have a chance to help someone else. That's all I'll ever ask."

One way or another, I guess I've been making payments on Doc's bills ever since.

There was a small downpayment during World War II. Quitting my job in a tax office, I donned the Red Cross uniform to work with war amputees at Walter Reed Hospital. The hospital's commanding general defined my assignment rather loosely when he said, "We need you, Viscardi. Don't ask me what your duties will be—maybe just walking around with your pants off. But we need you, that's certain."

I didn't walk around much with my pants off. I did show a lot of shattered young soldiers that they could walk around with their legs off. I tried to show them that life on artificial legs can still be a meaningful, exciting thing.

Many of those young men went out of the hospital willing to give it a try. Unfortunately, a lot of them wrote me later to say, "Hank, you lied to us. Nobody wants an amputee."

Hometown, America, had undone all the good work. People had welcomed the amputees back with parades and speeches; had offered them free cars, money and all the booze they could hold. But no jobs. Business is business. And, well, you know; it makes people kind of uncomfortable to have a cripple constantly around.

When it was over, I was discouraged, disgusted, ready to forget about other people's problems and solve my own. I landed a good job as assistant director of sports and special events at Mutual Broadcasting System. There I met a lovely young woman named Lucile and had the great good fortune to make her my wife. Soon I was stepping into the plush comfort of a skyscraper office as personnel director of a big New York textile firm. I was a Young Man with a Future. The past seemed behind me, the years of hardship and humiliation all neatly tucked out of sight.

I almost got away with it.

Then the phone rang one day, and Doc Yanover's bill came due again. This time it was an outfit called Just One Break. A new organization with exciting new ideas about helping the disabled. It had the support of people like Eleanor Roosevelt and Bernard Baruch. They wanted me to serve as executive director.

It offered a third of the salary I was making, and three times as much work, and I thought of a dozen good reasons for saying no. My always understanding Lucile took me off the hook.

"Hank," she said, "you want this thing, don't you? Let's do it."

Just One Break (J.O.B. we called it) was affiliated with Dr. Howard Rusk's world-famous rehabilitation institute at New York University-Bellevue Hospital. It was the job-hunting end of Dr. Rusk's bed-to-job program for restoring disabled people to normal life. I collected a staff of one, requisitioned a cubbyhole office at Bellevue, and plunged in.

My days and nights were filled with phone calls, interviews, an endless round of talks on the lunch-and-lecture circuit of civic clubs and business groups. The job applications from disabled workers poured in at a staggering rate. The job offers came slower—but they came.

Sometimes we sold the idea that a particular disability could be used to advantage. Like the young Navy vet who had lost a hand. He did fine in the kitchen of a big hotel. He could slip his steel hook into scalding water and fish out dishes the other workers couldn't touch.

More often, the disability didn't matter. An accountant in a wheelchair can be just as efficient as one in a swivel chair. A bit more efficient, perhaps, because he doesn't stroll over to the water cooler every few minutes to trade jokes with the boys. A blind girl is not a bit disqualified from taking dictation or answering a phone. It was surprising how hard it was sometimes to get that point across.

Often we failed. I remember Max Livermore, a keen-minded young chemist who was hit by shellfire on Normandy Beach. Max recovered nicely, he was really not disabled at all, except that a few nerves were irreparably severed. Unhappily, those nerves were in his face. His expression was permanently twisted into a hideous grimace.

"It isn't that *I* would mind having him around," one personnel director told me, "but you know, Mr. Viscardi, we have a good many girls working here. They are apt to be sensitive."

I blew up. "Fortunately for Max," I said, "his wife isn't that kind of sensitive. She tells me she didn't marry a face."

It was a good answer, but Max didn't get the job.

At other times I had to protect the disabled from human vultures. Sweatshop factories in firetrap tenements were all too willing to take crippled workers. They fattened on people who were too broke and beaten to argue terms. There were outfits, too, that thrived on thinly disguised professional begging. They hired the lame, the halt and the blind to peddle useless, overpriced gimcracks from door to door. But these angle boys were only a nuisance. They laid off J.O.B. applicants when they found out that I always checked.

The biggest problem was sheer numbers. We placed more than a thousand disabled people in jobs they were equipped to fill. For every one we placed, however, a dozen clamored to be put on our list. For every one we listed, a hundred needed help. We were trying to solve a national problem from a little two-by-four office with one phone and a couple of desks. I felt like King Canute when he tried to roll back the tides with a bailing bucket.

About this time I heard that some disabled veterans were planning to start their own shop in upstate New York. I got all stirred up. Maybe this was the beginning of an answer. It would show, at least, what disabled workers could do. For weeks I raced back and forth, driving four and five hours a night, trying to help the veterans get started. Eventually I withdrew in bitter disappointment. These boys had the right idea, but they were wrong in one crucial detail. They insisted on starting at the top of the ladder.

The vets planned to raise more than $200,000, equip

a fine new rehabilitation center complete with swimming pool and treatment rooms, and bring industry in to guarantee their contracts and pay. I begged them to be practical. "Start small," I said. "Think about work now, and maybe the swimming pool will come later. And forget that stuff about guaranteed pay. In business, like war, you have to take risks." But they couldn't see it. They raised a good deal of money, opened with a bang, and closed with a whimper a few months later.

The idea they had planted kept sticking in my mind. Done right, it might work. I found myself making more trips, more speeches; talking now about community shops. Lots of towns were interested. But something always happened to queer the deal.

I recall the earnest social worker who bobbed up in opposition at one town meeting. "Suppose," she said, "there was another depression? The disabled people would be hit first. They would only be out of work again."

I couldn't follow her thinking. Work *now* seemed better to me than no work ever. Surely there are some risks worth taking.

I began to suspect that some of the professional workers were like the gimcrack companies that hired beggars. They lived off cripples. Unconsciously, perhaps, they didn't want to see this problem solved.

I was going around and around, running faster and faster, getting madder and madder at more and more people. When I began to bolt my food and tumble in my bed at night, Lucile tried to exert her calming influence.

"Hank, honey," she said gently, "you've got to slow down. You're working too hard."

"No," I said, "you're wrong. I'm not working hard enough."

How could I rest when so many were begging for the right to work?

It seemed so plain to me that there were no disabled people—only people with varying degrees of ability at varying tasks. Why couldn't I make it plain to others? More and more I yearned for a shop where the so-called disabled could display their abilities for everybody to see.

I was in that kind of mood when a young man named Arthur Nierenberg hobbled into my office at J.O.B. He had a problem, like all the others. And he was plagued by the same idea that was keeping me awake nights.

CHAPTER TWO

RASH PROMISE

He came slowly, on crutches, a big scrapbook clutched crab fashion under one powerful shoulder. His knuckles showed white with the effort when he eased his powerful torso into the chair.

"I want a job," he said. "Any kind of a job. I'll work for nothing, just for the chance to prove myself."

I knew Arthur Nierenberg's case history already, thanks to my secretary, but I leafed through his scrapbook with the appearance of fresh discovery. I thought he needed a little time to compose himself.

Art was 24. He'd had polio at the age of two and a half, and had struggled ever since with two paralyzed legs and one partially paralyzed arm. His jacket, I knew, concealed a body brace which supported his spine. He had a high school diploma, and two years of college. He was trying to support a wife and child on a part time job, which paid him $21 a week.

The scrapbook added another dimension. Young Nierenberg was pictured at work in his children's furniture shop, set up on money borrowed from his father. I saw snapshots of the wheelchair he'd made for himself, the jigs and other devices he had developed to compensate for his paralysis.

He used his hands well, I surmised. His head, too.

"This looks interesting," I said to him now. "Why did you give it up?"

"I went broke." He put it bluntly, with no apology for having tried and failed.

"How much did you lose?"

"All my father had—$5,800," he said ruefully.

I liked this guy. He sat uncomfortably but not self-consciously, his withered legs dangling from a chair that was not cut to his size. The set of his shoulders, the firm line of his chin and mouth conveyed a stubborn strength. He looked straight at me with his keen dark eyes.

I veered away from the subject of the shop that failed. "Okay," I conceded. "So you need a job."

"I sure do." He hesitated a moment, then plunged on. "What I really want is to run another shop. I'd know more about it this time. I'd be able to figure costs, prices, things like that. I'd like to try it again—and I'd like to hire other disabled people, give them a chance."

"Maybe we can get together," I said. "I'm going to start a shop like that. I'll need a foreman."

My own words startled me. I didn't know I was going to say it until it came spilling out. When I started talking, though, I knew that the thought had been growing for a long, long time.

Me start the shop? Well, why not? Somebody had to do it. Somebody had to prove once and for all that the disabled were willing and able to work. Maybe it was time for Viscardi to quit cheerleading and grab the ball.

I couldn't work it out, though, with this eager young man staring at me across the desk. And he couldn't support his wife and child on my still half-formed dream.

"This is all very tentative," I told him. "Let's wait and see. Meantime, I know someone at the Servo-mechanisms electronic plant. Perhaps I can place you on their production line."

Much later, Art told me that it took him twenty-five tortuous minutes to negotiate the long corridor from Bellevue's entrance to my office door. He went back in five minutes, he said, with feet and crutches flying.

I didn't have the funds to establish a shop. But I thought now that I knew how to get financial backing. This time I'd go to businessmen.

I hit the lunch-and-lecture circuit again. Business clubs, professional organizations, Chambers of Commerce banquets—wherever two or more people were gathered together, it seemed, there was Viscardi standing up after the rubber chicken and green peas to deliver his speech.

Fired with a bright vision of what this shop could be, I talked and talked and talked. . . . We'd throw out the old insulting notion that disabled people should be protected and supervised like backward children. We'd dispense, too, with charity drives and professional hand holders. We'd run a real shop, in short; a place where men and women could earn a decent living doing useful work.

It wouldn't cost much. A little capital to set it up. After that, it would pay for itself. Even show a profit. We'd have a demonstration unit that could change America's whole thinking on this problem of the disabled worker.

Over and over I pounded at the theme that this was the kind of help disabled people wanted most. "They are crying out," I said, "for the right to be the same as others. They want to be considered as the ordinary people they really are; each with his individual capacities and limitations; each with qualities to compensate for extremes of physical suffering."

The speech went over big. There was a drumfire of applause after almost every luncheon, a big round of handshakes and congratulations, sometimes a glowing writeup in the club bulletin or local paper. Everybody agreed that it was a great idea.

And then, nothing. Everybody thought it was a great idea for somebody else to get behind.

Every few weeks I'd get a phone call from Art Nierenberg. He was at Servomechanisms now. Doing fine, thanks. He'd had two raises in the first month. But he still had the bug about a workshop for disabled people.

"How about it," he'd ask. "Are you still going to start that shop?"

"Sure, I'm going to start a shop. It takes a little time. . . . No, I haven't found a backer yet. . . . Keep in touch, Art. I'll let you know if anything breaks."

Then I'd go out and make another speech.

A few people did more than applaud. One of them was Don Weller, an intense, idealistic young public relations man. Don seemed to know everybody and belong to everything and he appointed himself a sort of one-man booster club and booking agency for Hank Viscardi. When I was ready to quit, he'd pump me full of confidence again, and line up another date.

"Don," I said finally, "I'm getting sick of it. What's the use? I talk and talk and nothing happens."

"Yeah, I know." He traced an idle pattern on the tablecloth at the all-night coffeeshop where we were recuperating from my latest burst of oratory. "I think," he added, "that I know what's wrong. You get them all fired up. Then they go back to their offices, and the whole thing dissipates before anybody has a chance to act.

"Now, suppose we change the routine. Next time, we'll plant a guy in the audience. As soon as you finish, he'll jump up and say, 'What can we do to help?' Don't you see, Hank?" A mischievous grin was tugging at the corner of Don's mouth. "This guy asks, 'What can we do?' You tell them. Before they know what's happening, you'll have them hooked."

How could I quit on this guy when he wouldn't quit trying?

"Okay, Don. We'll take a crack at it. One more speech. The next invitation I get, we'll plant your stooge and see what happens."

Don's grin was undisguised now. "Matter of fact, Hank, you already have the invitation. A Rotary Club out at Hempstead, Long Island. It's all lined up for lunch next week."

More rubber chicken and green peas. . . .

It was a beautiful day. Fat, puffy little clouds scudded across a sparkling sky as I entered the suburban golf club where the Rotarians were scheduled to meet. I paused in the lobby to sniff a big bowl of multi-colored tulips. I knew I was stalling. I was tense, coiled up, half-afraid to walk through the next door and face the test of another audience.

"Mr. Viscardi?" I turned, and a personable, business-like young man held out his hand. "I'm Charlie Langdon, program director. If you'll come with me—they're waiting."

As I followed Langdon down the long dining hall, I glanced out the huge French windows and saw a gay foursome of young women striding energetically toward the golf links beyond. I felt suddenly that my own stiff-legged mechanical gait was unbearably clumsy.

"Stage fright," I scolded myself. But it was more than that. I had made up my mind that this would be my last appeal. It had to be good.

We glanced at the menu. It suggested planked shad. The thought of food tied a fresh knot in my stomach. "Later," I said, then sat with my hands gripped together under the table.

Talk eddied around me. I made no attempt to respond. Soon I would be introduced and, thanks to my aluminum legs, I could stand up, a man among men, and be listened to. But would they really hear and understand? Could I make them understand?

"Blessed Mother," I prayed, "give me the words. Help me to do this for my people and I will dedicate what we do to you."

I was aware of coffee cups being pushed back, of cigars being lighted. The chairman was rising to go through the familiar routine of introduction. I was on.

I can't tell you today what I said. I spoke from the heart, about the thing nearest my heart. It rolled out of me in a great torrent of emotion and fierce conviction. There was silence when I finished, and then a long sigh went through the room. I sat down, exhausted. A big burst of applause told me that the audience was with me—so far.

"Mr. Viscardi." A stocky, white-haired man bobbed up at a back table. "What can we do about this problem? I mean, right here in Hempstead?"

Don's plant was doing his stuff.

I jerked myself back to my feet. "If you really want to tackle this problem, you can help me start a shop. You can put up some cash."

That did it. Questions came flying from every table. How much would it cost? How would it operate? How many disabled were there? What kind of work could they do? When could we start?

When the meeting broke up, a dozen men pushed forward to continue the discussion. One man came up to say that he couldn't stay, and then stayed. We talked costs, contracts, locations, manpower for nearly an hour. I ordered a sandwich—I could eat now—and munched happily while the discussion flowed on. Occasionally I put in a word about what the shop should *not* be. No paternalism, no charity drives, no subsidies. Workers would be employees, not pets. Our backers would be investors, not donors; the money would be paid back with interest out of shop earnings.

They liked it. "You'll get the money," several men

assured me. "The executive committee will have to rule on it—but that's just a formality."

I didn't feel clumsy when I rose to leave. I could look through the big windows now without envy for the lithe young golfers striding across the course. Who wants to play golf when the world is so full of exciting things to do?

"Mr. Viscardi." A man grabbed my arm at the door. "I'm Bill Effinger. Couldn't get a word in edgewise in all this hubbub, but I think I can give you some work. And I know just the place for your plant."

Bill was president of Berkley Models, a West Hempstead firm that made model airplanes and other craft toys. He was planning to bring out a new item, he said, and he wanted to give our shop a crack at the assembly work. It sounded fine. The location he had in mind was an empty garage, right next door to his place. We jumped in my car, and went to see it.

The garage was bare, some might say grim; but it had a good cement floor and solid cement block walls. It was dry and heated. Windows on three sides and several skylights in the high raftered roof provided ample light and ventilation. And it was near a bus stop. People on crutches could get to work.

There were no furnishings or facilities of any kind, not much of a washroom. But that could be fixed.

"It'll do," I said. "In fact, it's swell. How much do they want?"

"Milton Bedell owns it. He runs that coal yard just across the street. Let's go ask him."

Bedell wanted $195 a month. Not a bad price. He warned me, though, that several others were interested. We'd have to hurry.

I don't know what the clouds over Long Island looked like when I broke away finally and headed for home. I was riding on a beautiful cloud of my own.

With the shop in sight, I began looking around for jobs to do.

I heard that Sperry Gyroscope Company was letting out sub-contracts for electronic assembly and packaging. It was skilled work at good pay, the kind of thing people in wheelchairs could do easily with the proper training. I arranged to call on Preston Bassett, who was Sperry's president at the time.

I was surprised, pleasantly so, when I was ushered into Bassett's office. I'd expected to meet a brisk, coldly efficient "executive type." I found instead an unassuming man, quiet, infinitely kind and human. His hands were working hands—he looked somehow as though he had just laid down well-loved tools.

I found myself pouring out my heart to him. I told him of my mounting frustrations at J.O.B., of my belief that a pilot shop would help disabled people everywhere by proving that they can work and earn. He listened raptly, obviously moved.

"How much do you want me to give?" he asked.

"I don't want you to give anything. What I want is a chance to do some of your subcontracting work— that and your belief in me while I'm getting started."

"Well, Mr. Viscardi," he smiled, "it's not hard to have faith, when you have so much yourself."

Bassett called in Carl Holschuh, his executive vice president. Holschuh was all business. He listened with genuine interest, betraying no emotion as he started asking questions.

"Where is your plant, Mr. Viscardi?"

I explained about the garage.

"You haven't rented it yet?"

"Well, no; not exactly. You see, I'm still waiting on Rotary. I'm sure they'll come through."

"I see."

This man with his careful, probing questions was beginning to make me feel uncomfortable.

Bassett came to my rescue. "I'm sure you'll work it out, Mr. Viscardi. Let's talk again when your arrangements have jelled."

Every few days I checked with Milton Bedell to see if the garage deal was still open. Art Nierenberg kept calling me to ask when the shop would be ready to start. At any moment I expected to hear from Rotary.

I phoned the club president two or three times, but he was out. He didn't answer my calls. When the days slipped into weeks and still no word, I began to have a gnawing doubt. I called Jack Coffey, a young lawyer who was secretary of the club.

"Gee, Hank," he said, "I don't know. It should be all settled by now, but I haven't heard a thing. I'll find out and buzz you right back."

Ten minutes later he was back on the wire. I knew from his tone that the news was bad.

"Brace yourself for this, Hank. They turned it down."

"Turned it down? Why, Jack? Why?"

"I'm sorry, Hank. Everything was all set until they brought in a cautious old lawyer who advised against it. He warned them that they'd be responsible if the shop went bankrupt. He said Rotary might get sued if a worker was hurt. The committee backed out."

"Jack, what's the matter with these people?" My voice was rising. "Doesn't anybody have any nerve?"

"Hank," he said, "I'm terribly sorry. I thought it was a great idea. I still do. If you decide to go ahead with this thing on your own, I'll help in any way I possibly can."

So I was back where I started. All the trips and speeches, the countless hours of talking and planning, and then some lawyer I'd never met stepped in to kill it with a word. Too risky. It might fail. Not a thought, apparently, that it might also succeed. I was building up to a real boil when the phone rang again.

It was Milton Bedell this time. He had another prospect who wanted the garage. He couldn't hold it for me
any longer. When he heard that I'd lost my sponsor,
he sympathized and started to hang up.

"Wait a minute," I said. "Rotary backed out of this
thing. I'm not backing out. Will you let me have that
place on a short-term lease?"

He hesitated. He wanted to give me a break. Then
he said he would. Under the circumstances, though,
he'd have to have two months' rent in advance, and a
month's security.

"My check," I said, "will be in the mail."

Defiantly, I scrawled the check, and tried not to look
at the shrinking balance. Somebody has to get this thing
out of the talking stage, I told myself, and Viscardi
seems to be elected.

I knew it was a reckless gesture. I didn't have money
enough to buy equipment, meet payrolls, or do any of
the things that must be done to transform an empty
building into a shop. By grabbing the lease I had gained
a little time—but time for what? Then a call from
Preston Bassett brought a fresh surge of hope. He
wanted me to meet a friend of his, a banker named
Arthur Roth, who might furnish private backing for
the shop.

"I've told him about your idea," Bassett said. "He's
interested. He wants to hear more."

I checked around a little, tried to get a line on Roth.

He was, I learned, a very successful, very conservative banker. The kind of man who drives a Cadillac and then walks to work after parking blocks from his place of business because the bank's free parking lot is for the use of customers.

When I met him I quickly gathered other impressions. He was tall, thin-faced, almost patrician looking. But his eyes were warm and expressive, his tone was soft-spoken. Restless energy was betrayed in the way he fiddled constantly with a pencil, now twirling it, now tapping it against the table, now jotting down a word or figure on a note pad and underlining it with a quick, sharp little stroke.

I told my story. Bassett helped by feeding me leading questions. Roth listened, never interrupting until I was done. Then in that soft voice of his he came at once to the heart of the question.

"How much capital would your shop require?"

"Perhaps $5,000. . ." My words were half hope, half question.

He shook his head. "I doubt if you could do it on that. This is a new venture; you'd run into all kinds of unusual expenses. You might see several thousand dollars go down the drain before you could turn a productive wheel."

"Mr. Roth," I said desperately. "I'll be glad to accept more backing if I can get it. But I'm going ahead with whatever I get. I'll open this shop if I can keep it open for only a week."

Another shake of the head rejected that notion. "I don't believe in making bad investments," he said, "not even for good causes. If this shop is to be started at all, it should have a reasonable chance to survive." He considered a moment, jotted a figure on his scratch pad, underlined it with that characteristic stroke. "Tell you what I'll do. I'll guarantee up to $4,000 providing you can get other backers to come in for a matching amount. That should give us enough to get going."

My heart jumped when he said "us." After long search I had found a man who wanted to buy shares in my dream.

When I contacted Nierenberg I laid it out in stark detail.

"I've got a prospective backer," I said, "and a place to work in, and one or two job possibilities that might come through. A few people want to help. But that's about all. I'll have to scramble like crazy for money, for work, for everything. It's going to be a big gamble all the way. Do you still want in?"

"If you're betting on it," Art said, "I'm willing to bet on you. When do we start?"

CHAPTER THREE

YOU'VE GOT TO START SOMEWHERE

The garage wasn't really big. It seemed vast and terribly empty, though, on the day we opened for business.

Art Nierenberg made a lonely little island in the sea of floor space. He perched in his homemade wheelchair behind a battered old desk salvaged from Bedell's nearby coal yard. Near the desk was a borrowed drafting board. There was a telephone on the cement block wall, and a flyswatter beside it. That was the total equipment.

For money there was $4,000 put up by Roth and his friends, plus a matching amount I had managed to raise from other businessmen. But that could go fast. A mistake or two in pricing jobs, a little delay in finding work to do, and this dream would be buried in the dusty archives of bankruptcy court.

27

As I stood in the drafty old building, and took stock of our chances, I thought wryly that at least it would be a perfect experiment. We were trying to prove that handicapped people could earn a place for themselves. And we seemed to be starting with just about every handicap in the books.

Art's gamble in a way was bigger than mine.

I was paying him only $50 a week—more than I could afford but less than he needed to live. He was working weekends in his father's butcher shop to scratch out the little extra he had to have to get by.

He was living with his wife, Rhoda, and their baby in an unheated summer bungalow. With winter coming, he would have to move soon. If the shop failed, he and his family were in real trouble.

"We'll manage somehow," he assured me. "We always do."

Art busied himself checking blueprints of the model toys Bill Effinger was turning out next door. He went over them inch by inch, looking for shortcuts in the assembly job. We didn't have a contract with Effinger yet, and we weren't sure that we could do the job at his price, but Art thought he might find a way to make it pay.

Charlie Langdon, the friend I'd met at Rotary, dropped in every morning to provide Art with a few bright moments of coffee and conversation. Charlie brought the coffee in paper cups and, since we didn't have chairs, he'd sit on an empty crate. When Charlie was tied up at his real estate office, his wife would come. It got to be a ritual.

The rest of the time Art sat in his wheelchair swatting the thick swarming flies while he waited for the phone to ring.

I was trying to make the phone ring. With orders for work. I was wrestling, too, with the paper work and planning that a new venture requires.

The planning sessions met evenings, usually at the garage. Half a dozen of our official and unofficial sponsors participated almost every night—businessmen who were lending us the money to get started, and others who lent their brains and moral support. We perched on crates, and spent hours sometimes batting ideas around.

We gave a lot of thought to choosing a name. I was determined that it would not include the term "Disabled" or "Handicapped," or any pity-seeking word. To trade on sympathy would destroy the whole point of our effort.

"Let's forget the disabilities," I said at one session. "We've got to start thinking about what we can do, not what we can't. We should stress our abilities. . . . "

"Abilities, Inc." That was it.

We set it up as a non-profit membership corporation, with Viscardi as president and chairman of the board.

An advisory board was made up of Preston Bassett, Arthur Roth and other business and community leaders.

For directors we chose successful men who had licked the disability problem in their personal lives. That was to hammer home the Abilities point, to prove that you can't measure a whole man by some fixed number of arms, legs or working nerve cells.

One of the directors was Orin Lehman, an old friend from J.O.B. A brilliant young man, and member of the famous Lehman family, he'd lost one leg and had the other shattered in World War II. Orin was the man who introduced me to J.O.B. I figured I owed him a tough assignment.

H. Chester Swezey of Eastport, L. I., said he'd serve, too. Blind since birth, he'd grown wealthy in the trucking business. Swezey was in his seventies, but still young-minded enough to give a hearing to new ideas.

James Golden of Brooklyn made a third. A slim, graying man, limping for fifty years as a result of childhood polio, he employed others who limped and hobbled in his Empire Mailing Service. Jim started his shop as an adjunct to the Brooklyn Bureau of Charities, but the bureau was horrified when he suggested that the operation should show a profit and pay a competitive wage. So he pulled out, established his own firm, and continued to hire the disabled on a business basis.

We'd planned to have only disabled men as directors but we had to stretch the point when we came to

Attorney Jack Coffey. Young, healthy Coffey—he'd been one of my real boosters at the Rotary. He'd pitched in to help in a dozen ways after the Rotary deal fell through. I just couldn't get along without his quick legal mind and eager interest in the Abilities idea.

"Dammit, Jack," I said finally, "there must be something wrong with you. There's something wrong with everybody. We'll charge you with dandruff and count you in."

We were a nonprofit organization—shop earnings would be poured back into programs to help the disabled—and on that basis I thought we were entitled to exemption from corporate taxes. At Roth's suggestion I talked it over with Joe Landow, an accountant, who became my great friend and financial advisor.

Joe spent several days checking regulations and reported back that an exemption seemed doubtful. We were something new, an organization that sought to be both private business and public service. Our request would require a ruling from the Internal Revenue Department, and that would take at least a year.

I couldn't wait a year. Not now.

We needed a specialist in tax matters. Orin Lehman suggested Isadore Sach, the tax expert at the banking firm of Lehman Brothers, and one of the best in the business. Joe and I made a date to see him.

Sach was a gray haired, scholarly man, who sat behind a huge desk cluttered with legal tomes. He peered through heavy glasses and his head jutted forward from his shoulders as though he were seeking something. He listened graciously while Joe and I explained our mission. Then he swiveled around, plucked a volume from a dusty shelf, and read intently. We waited.

"You can do it," he advised finally. "It is unusual but I believe it can be done. Do you know anyone in Washington?"

We didn't.

"This kind of problem calls for special handling," Sach said. "It should be settled high up, on a person-to-person basis." He thought for a moment. "Randolph Paul might be your man. He had an important Treasury Department position in the last administration; now he practices law in Washington."

Sach leaned forward, pressed a button, spoke into his office intercom. "Get Paul on the wire," he said crisply.

And so I went to see Paul.

Paul's Washington office was a converted home. From the outside it looked like one of the smaller embassies; inside it was furnished with quiet elegance. The man himself had the solid, successful air of a corporate lawyer.

Fascination was plainly written on Paul's face as I outlined the Abilities dream. When I had finished he asked a few incisive questions.

"You plan to make a profit, Mr. Viscardi. Yet you seek a nonprofit tax exemption?"

"Yes," I explained. "The shop must make money to prove that disabled people can compete in the business world. But shop earnings will not go into private pockets. The profits will be invested in teaching, training, medical programs, public education—all the things that need to be done in rehabilitation."

He nodded, picked up a phone, got through to someone in Treasury. There was a brisk exchange of pleasantries, then Paul got down to business. "This afternoon would be fine," I heard him say. "We'll be there promptly at two o'clock."

Paul glanced at his watch as he hung up. "We'll have to move right along," he observed, "but I think we just have time to make it." He summoned his secretary, began at once to transcribe our plea into the complex language of a legal brief.

The Treasury conference that afternoon seemed to go well. No commitment from anyone. But encouraging remarks. Much interest. They would consider it and let us know.

Later, seeing me off at the airport, Paul told me I had good reason to hope. "Those people believed in you," he said. "That counts for a lot. There's a heart in Washington if you know where to find it."

I held out my hand to say goodbye. "You'll send me your bill?"

"No—I've been repaid already. I'm used to handling cases where all that's involved is a few million dollars. It's not every day I can help someone do a thing like this."

A week later I received a letter from the Treasury Department. It was written in the jawbreaking jargon of official Washington but to me it read like a poem. Our request was granted.

There remained the problem of getting work. Already we'd used up a month getting financed and organized. So far we hadn't made even a first dollar to frame on our bare walls.

We had counted on model airplane work but that job still wasn't ready to go. We weren't sure we could make it pay if we got it. And nothing else was in sight.

Jim Golden on our board of directors suggested that I try his mailing service idea. That would put me in competition with him, of course, but he waved it aside. "There's work enough for both of us," he said, then added with a sardonic wink: "Don't worry about Jim Golden, boy. You'll have to hurry early and late to put me out of business."

Jim showed me through his shop, explained the fine points of the operation, and described the advantages. A mailing service required very little equipment or training. The work is steady. Profit is small, but it's a living. "You could," he said, "do worse. Why don't you try it?"

At Jim's suggestion I hustled around to see the circulation manager of a leading national magazine. The magazine's tremendous mailing would keep us busy if we could handle only a little of it.

The magazine people agreed at once. There was a slight obstacle—a man in Bellport, New York, had the mailing contract—but they would ask him to farm out a small piece of the job to us. Anxious to close the deal, I jumped back in the car and drove another sixty miles to see the contractor.

I needn't have rushed. The man in Bellport turned me down. It wasn't a flat no—he couldn't take that attitude in view of the magazine's request—but his lingering no was just as final. He said he didn't have anything for me just now. He promised vaguely that he would keep me in mind. I was sure that he wouldn't.

I started to get sore, and then I remembered the theme song of Viscardi's favorite speech. The disabled don't want favors, just a chance to compete on equal terms. Okay, no favors. This man didn't have to cut us in on his business. We had to cut ourselves in somewhere by doing something a little better or faster than anyone else.

Maybe we should jump right into electronic assembly. That was a tough field, but it had tempted me from the first. It was skilled work, at excellent pay, and a man could do it without legs or even eyes if he had good fingers. Industry didn't believe that, of course, but industry could be shown. If the doubting Thomases could only see what I had seen so often. . . .

Suddenly I realized that I could make them see it. I knew of a community workshop at Binghamton, New York, that would serve well enough for demonstration purposes. IBM was its main sponsor. It was a sheltered shop, not the kind of thing we wanted to organize, but that didn't detract from the fine work the disabled were doing there. I could take my prospects to Binghamton, get them fired up with the possibilities of this thing, and sign them to contracts before they cooled off.

I'd start with Sperry Gyroscope. Bassett was there; I knew he'd give the idea a hearing.

A call to Sperry went right through to Bassett. He fell in enthusiastically, corralled four of his top brass, and requisitioned a company plane for the trip. He suggested a date of Thursday, July 24, and I cleared the whole thing with the Binghamton people. We were all set. I was sure it would work. I could almost feel the crisp crinkle of a Sperry contract in my pocket.

And then I received a call that would have buckled my legs under me if they had built any knee action into Viscardi's aluminum pins. The caller was Dr. James Farrar, medical director of a large New York manufacturing company. He reminded me that I was scheduled to speak at a conference on industrial medicine in Saratoga. The date was for Thursday, July 24.

"Thursday!" I said in shocked disbelief. The Thursday I was counting on, the day when I would show Sperry executives an idea in action. The voice on the phone was going on, saying friendly, inconsequential things, but I wasn't listening. I was sick.

Why wasn't this on my calendar? Then I recalled that Dr. Farrar hadn't been sure of the date when he asked me to speak. Perhaps he had forgotten to confirm it. Perhaps he had notified me, and in the hurly burly of launching Abilities I had forgotten to put it down. It didn't matter. What did matter was that I was stuck with conflicting appointments at the worst possible moment.

What could I say? Jim Farrar is a prince of a guy. His company was a potential customer if Abilities got started. Certainly the doctors, personnel directors and others attending the conference needed to hear what I had to say. In all decency, I could not, three days before their conference, let them down.

How to tell Bassett? What kind of a businessman would he think I was, not keeping my appointments straight? I cursed myself and phoned him. He wasn't rough with me, he never is with anyone, but he was sort of remote. "Well, don't worry, Mr. Viscardi," he said. "We'll arrange another date sometime."

But of course I worried. I was still sick with worry when I kept the convention date.

I got caught with my pants down at that conference. And in more ways than one.

Things started to go wrong on the trip to Saratoga. I was supposed to fly upstate with Jim and his wife, Jane, in their little private airplane. One look at the plane and I knew it wasn't built with Viscardi in mind. There were two seats in front, two behind, and practically no space in between. Since my knees don't bend much, I couldn't squeeze in.

For a wild moment I thought, "I don't have to go after all." Then I knew that I did. And, anyway, I had already cancelled my big reason for staying behind.

"Get in, Jane," I said, "and don't look back. It's a good thing your husband's along because I have to take off my pants."

Jane and Jim took their places and gazed gravely ahead while I recovered my trousers, unhooked my legs, and deposited what was left of Viscardi on the shallow back seat. It was a ridiculous position but I was too numb to care. Detaching my legs was after all only a small inconvenience. What hurt was wrenching my mind and heart away from that other trip, with Sperry.

If the take-off was undignified, the landing was worse. As we touched down at Saratoga, a reception committee came rushing forward to meet the plane. There were ladies among them. And Viscardi was in no shape to be received.

"Jim!" I shouted. "Jane! Get out there quick and stall them off. Give me five minutes to do my fire drill stuff." As I flailed around getting reassembled, I reflected grimly that at least I was setting some sort of record. Medical conferences are not noted for high jinks. This surely was the first time that a speaker arrived in his underwear.

To top it off, my speech was a flop. I couldn't move the audience; couldn't sense any spark or feel any answering warmth. These people really didn't seem to know what it was like to live crippled and rejected, and suddenly I didn't have the words to tell them. Listless faces gazed up at me as I struggled desperately with my thoughts. Bored feet shuffled in the aisles. Limp hands responded at the end with the most awful sound a speaker can hear—polite applause.

Maybe it was my fault. Maybe I was so wrapped up in worry and self-doubt that I couldn't make contact. Or maybe the conferees regarded the whole thing as a bore. They might have put me on, reluctantly, as a favor to Jim. To fill a blank spot in the program. That thought really rocked me.

Exhaustion intervened then, and I quit thinking at all. On the flight back, I fell into a restless, troubled sleep, my legs once again in my lap.

The conference fiasco taught me a lesson. I shoved everything else aside now, and settled down to a single-minded search for work.

The quest led to Servomechanisms. That company

farmed out electronic jobs, and we had the makings of a useful contact there. Servo's production men knew Nierenberg's work, and liked it, from the three months he had spent on their bench. I got in touch with Nierenberg's old boss, and asked him for an introduction to the company's purchasing agent, Arthur Bartlett.

Bartlett was a hard man to see. Viscardi by now was a hard man to avoid seeing. I staked out a position in the Servo waiting room and laid siege to him for three days. When patience failed, I tried shock tactics and demanded to see the head of the firm.

"Look here," I told the receptionist. "I don't have to wait like this to see Bernard Baruch. If Mr. Bartlett can't see me, please take my card to the boss."

It worked. Doors opened, people found time where they had been too busy before. And Bartlett, when I met him, proved nice enough. He told me that Servo was swamped with rush orders for the Korean War. Perhaps we could help.

Perhaps! I was certain of it. I would guarantee delivery and quality. I bore down hard on the fact that my shop boss was Servo trained, and held my breath for fear he'd ask how many men I had. He didn't ask, so I didn't have to explain.

I walked out with my first contract.

The order was for 340 sets of upper and lower harnesses—part of the firing mechanism for Sabrejet fighter planes. It was marked ASAP, meaning "as soon as possible." I found myself savoring the prospect that we'd have to beat our brains out to get it done on time. After weeks of worry over nothing to do, this kind of problem would be pure pleasure.

The terms were a source of pleasure, too. Our first order was for the fat sum of $1,870.

I rushed home to tell Lucile.

It was late when I reached home but the whole family was up and waiting.

Lucile sat in the big easy chair looking serenely beautiful. The children, Donna and Nina, were scampering about as though they sensed somehow that big events were afoot which allowed them to violate the usual strict rules about bedtime.

Lucile's parents—Poppy and Nana we called them—were there, too. They looked a bit anxious.

There was proper jubilation when Viscardi announced his big news. Lucile gave me a victory hug. "Oh, darling," she said, "I'm so glad. This makes it a perfect day. Now, I have some news, too. I think you and I had better start for the hospital right away."

There was the rushing business of going to the hospital. Then the waiting business in the corridors. It seemed a long, long wait. In the small hours of the morning a doctor finally emerged from the delivery room.

"Congratulations," he said. "You have a beautiful little girl."

We named her Lydia, and she is as different from the other two as they are from each other.

CHAPTER FOUR

A LEG TO STAND ON

With work to do, we began hiring men.

We didn't need to place a "Help Wanted" ad. The disabled heard of us, and sought us out. Hardly a day passed without adding to the little procession of the lame, the blind, the scarred and mangled who found their way to our door.

Choosing among them was not an easy task. Nearly two dozen begged for a chance; we had room at the moment for only three.

One of the applicants was a half-scared, half-eager kid named Horace Johnson. He was waiting one morning, leaning on crutches, when I came down to open the shop. As he followed me inside, I noted his stiff-legged,

43

uncertain gait. I guessed, correctly, that he was wearing long leg braces which lock at the knees. The effect is much like walking on stilts, only more awkward.

Horace's case history followed a familiar pattern. A polio victim, stricken at three, he had spent more than half of his life in hospital wards. Both legs were badly crippled, one arm partially so. His training was meager —what with time out for treatment he had finished only two years of high school—and his work record was worse. He'd held two jobs, and had been fired from both at the end of a week.

The bare chronology made him seem the worst kind of prospect. Looked at from another light, though, it suggested that his timid exterior hid a sturdy spirit. Horace had to be game, or he wouldn't still be trying.

"How well do you handle those crutches?" I asked.

"Not too bad, I guess. I can manage a block, maybe two blocks, if I take it slow and easy. Going up stairs, I have to crawl. . . . " He stopped suddenly, afraid that he was saying too much.

"You'd have a problem," I said, "in getting to work. From where you live, it takes more than an hour. You'd have to get on and off two buses, and walk between bus stops. That's a pretty tough trip."

"I made it this morning, didn't I?"

I couldn't answer the argument, so I gave him a job.

Another we hired was intense, serious young Bill Graham. He was paralyzed from the waist down, the consequence of a sniper's bullet in World War II. He had been hit, too, by something worse than a bullet. Like so many of the amputees I trained at Walter Reed, he had discovered that a shattered veteran is often "war surplus" when the shooting stops.

Bill wouldn't accept that verdict. Through long hours of tedious exercise, he built up what was left of his body. He learned to drive a car with special controls, thus freeing himself to come and go without depending upon others. He mastered a trade school course, became a skilled craftsman with precision tools. And then, for years, he tried vainly to find work. When he came to Abilities, at 27, he had never held another job.

Jim Rizzo was hired also. A wiry little man—I doubt that he weighed more than a hundred pounds—he had lost one arm and one leg in a construction accident.

Jim wore an artificial arm terminating in a steel claw, or hook, with two curved "fingers" held together by a rubber band. Across his shoulders was a complicated sling arrangement; it allowed him to manipulate the arm and claw by contracting his shoulder muscles. It was a clumsy apparatus, and Jim hated it. Almost invariably he parked his arm in the shop washroom when he went home at night.

Jim's leg was off at the hip. The right side of his body rested in a leather bucket to which an artificial leg was attached; the whole thing was fastened to his body by a padded steel belt around the waist. He couldn't sit com-

fortably—the gear jutted out at an awkward angle—
but when he locked his mechanical knee he could stand
for hours without fatigue. In effect he "sat" on the leg
as he would on a stool. Jim was the only employee who
could walk without aid. The boys called him "the leg
man" and assigned him to such extra duties as sweeping
out at night.

Art Nierenberg completed the roster. It made quite
a crew—four men with only five good arms among
them, only one good leg. But four stout-hearted men
just the same.

Nierenberg took charge as foreman. Some of my ad-
visors wanted me to bring in an outsider for this crucial
job, but I vetoed that. If we really believed in the
Abilities dream we had to stick with it all the way. If
success came, I wanted the whole world to know that
there wasn't a man in the place who hadn't done it the
hard way.

That, after all, was what we were trying to prove.

We didn't swing into production right away. In
launching Abilities, nothing was ever as simple as that.
Before we could work at all, we had to transform an
empty, poorly lighted building into the semblance of a
plant. And Viscardi had to take a very fast cram course
in electronic assembly.

My cram course instructor was E. U. Da Parma, a

bright young man at Sperry Gyroscope then, and now a vice-president. A very serious young man, yet with a capacity for quick, spontaneous laughter. His friends call him Uly. I met him through Bassett and sensed at once his instinctive understanding of the disability problem. He had, as I learned later, come to know disability through tragic experience of those close to him. He was to influence and guide me often in the years to come.

I confessed to Da Parma that I was in a pretty tight spot. I'd grabbed a harness contract because I had to grab something, yet I scarcely knew the difference between an electronic harness and the kind you hang on a horse. Now I had to produce—and I couldn't afford mistakes while learning.

"You can handle it," Da Parma assured me. "Stick to the specifications and you can't go wrong. But let's get together and talk it over."

We met the next evening at the garage. Da Parma brought two associates who had charge of Sperry's plant layout and wiring; Abilities was represented by myself and Nierenberg. We pulled up the old crates we were still using for chairs, and big business sat down to tell little business how it's done.

Those boys really covered the ground. Not just harness production, but problems of heat, light, power, equipment, materials, contract terms—the whole technique of small shop operation in the electronic field. In two or three hours they gave me a briefing I shall never forget. While we talked the Sperry men appraised our building with a professional eye. Before they left we had a rough sketch of a floor plan. Later Da Parma sent over one of his assistants to make a detailed layout.

Slowly the plant began to take shape. Nierenberg assembled four wooden workbenches, and placed them in aisles wide enough for wheelchair passage. Sperry gave us another bench, a discard, and some materials racks. Ford Instrument Company, a friendly rival with Sperry in helping us get started, sent over some old fluorescent lights. But we still lacked wiring, fuse boxes, switches. It would take more than $5,000 to do the job right.

James Carpenter who had joined our advisory board offered help in that. An active man in community affairs, he was a vice president of the Long Island Lighting Company. Like many others I met in this period, he was also a man with his own deeply personal reasons for belief in the Abilities idea. His only child, a daughter, was disabled. When Carpenter heard of our wiring problem he asked local electric contractors to get out their pencils and do "some figuring" on our job.

The contractors didn't stop at "some figuring." Twenty-five of them, all boss men who had not been on ladders in years, donned overalls and swarmed through the rafters of our plant. They worked an entire weekend, installed a magnificent job of wiring, and charged not a cent.

In every man's life, certain days stand out sharp-etched and separate from all the rest. Monday, August 25, 1952, was that kind of a day for me.

It was the day we finally started to work.

Laid out on the benches were soldering pots, a few crimping and wire skinning tools, great bundles of wire, and several sets of lacing boards. Our job was to assemble harnesses—they amount to prefabricated wiring units—for use in jet planes.

Rows of nails and cotter pins on the lacing boards outlined the path each piece of wire must follow. We had to strip and tin the wires, snake them into position, and lace them with cord so that they retained the design when lifted from the board.

A unit consisted of twenty or more wires, and became, when finished, a gnarled, intricately twisted "rope" about nine inches long and as thick as your thumb. The strands trailed off network fashion in many directions. It's known in the trade as a simple harness, and it proved simple enough when we got the hang of it. At the start, though, it seemed complex, difficult, heartbreakingly slow.

Horace Johnson was supposed to strip and tin the wires, but he couldn't hold them with his polio-paralyzed thumb, and he was soon in a lather. His fear of failure only made it worse. Twice before he had been fired in a hurry; this, he thought, was sure to end the same way. Nierenberg saw the state the boy was in.

"Look, kid," Art said, "you don't *have* to hold these things with your thumb. See how I do." He seized the wires expertly between his first two fingers. Horace followed suit. He was still slow and fumbling, but gradually he got the knack. Horace's weak hand presented another problem—he couldn't squeeze the lugging wrench—but we solved that by fastening one end of the wrench to the table. Then he just leaned on it.

Jim Rizzo was having his troubles, too. He was supposed to solder lugs on the wires, a task which requires a delicate touch. Working with one hand, his left hand at that, and with a poorly controlled hook, he kept dropping the lugs. He would swear in exasperation, rest the heavy hook on the bench for a moment, then try again.

Again it was Art who found the answer. He rummaged through some discarded packing materials, found a small box, and nailed it to the bench to serve as a platform. Jim could steady his hook now, and the splatter of lugs on the floor began to cease.

Bill Graham sat in his wheelchair and applied his two good hands to assembly and lacing. He handled it well once he learned the pattern. Art worked on that, too, when he wasn't wheeling up and down the line to instruct and inspect.

Art, in fact, was proving a natural leader in every respect. At noon the first day, he noted that Horace had failed to bring lunch. Horace insisted that he wasn't hungry, but was prevailed upon to share in the sandwiches. When it happened again the next day, and the next, Art called Horace aside.

"What's the problem?" he asked.

The problem was that Horace had all he could manage to get on and off buses. He couldn't handle his crutches and carry a lunch pail. An old Army knapsack which strapped to the shoulders proved the answer to that one.

Some other problems could not be solved, and so they were simply endured. Hot, dusty winds whipped through the shop when the big garage doors were open, a clammy heat enveloped the place when the doors were closed. Flies swarmed thick in either case. But so intent was the effort that such irritations passed almost unnoticed most of the time.

There was a brief moment of relaxation once a day when our friend, Charlie Langdon, paid his now traditional call with cartons of coffee under his arm. "Expanding, expanding, always expanding," he'd exclaim in mock awe as he passed out the containers. "I can remember when this was just a one-cup operation."

Art's former shop boss at Servo, a man known affectionately as Old Garcia, was a frequent visitor, too. Sometimes he offered a word of advice or encouragement; usually he just stood quietly, watching. Old Garcia had his reservations about our chances, I think, but he was rooting for us all the way. He was as troubled as we were when things went badly, as proud as we when we achieved a gain.

I was in and out of the shop, keeping one eye on operations and trying to line up the new jobs we'd need when this one was licked. If it was licked. For many anxious days that question hung in the balance.

The men adjusted to their problems, slowly at first, then with increasing confidence, but production still lagged far behind schedule. By competitive standards, we should have been turning out twenty sets of harness a day. We finished only twenty in the first two weeks.

Then all at once we started taking hold. We hit quota, held to it, finally topped it as the men molded themselves by sheer effort into a smooth working crew. We took on seven new employees, all disabled of course, and managed to teach them the system without breaking stride. In eight weeks, the job was done.

When we delivered the final lot, we found that we had set a record for quality. The job was perfect, not a single rejection. Servo's production foremen didn't think it was possible, and clustered in the receiving room to see for themselves. Old Garcia, eyes shining, led the cheering section on our behalf. "Good work," he kept saying. "Real good. Better than we do ourselves."

Good work. How sweet the sound of those two words!

Servo's purchasing department made the compliment

complete. They gave us another and larger harness order.

Abilities celebrated in its own way. The boys presented me with a sample harness, handsomely framed, for the fenced-off corner of the garage that I called my office. The typed label read: "An intrical component of the electronic gunsight mechanism of the Sabrejet fighter. First contract, Abilities, Inc."

I've never let anyone correct that garbled "integral." It's symbolic, I think, that they produced something they couldn't spell.

We had fourteen employees now. And several new jobs.

Sperry gave us a packaging assignment on 4,500 bags of assorted Air Force parts. Then two orders for tube brackets and socket assemblies. Not big contracts, but enough to keep us going.

The garage was a happy, busy place. The men in it felt useful, and needed, and they responded like plants to the sun. Jokes flowed across the workbenches, friendships grew, cheerful calls of "See you tomorrow" expressed the link which held them together.

Of course, it was not a quick and easy transition for all. There are lazy men on crutches, as well as off, and some men get used to being helpless and find it a habit hard to break. We had to fire two who wouldn't try.

We went a long way with others because they did try. Like one 18-year-old whom we'll call Bill. A victim of cerebral palsy, he'd fallen out of a window once, been hit by a car another time. His speech was impaired and his movements were almost totally uncoordinated.

We put Bill on bracket assembly, an easy job. Brackets are holders for electronic tubes. Bill's task was to apply fiber glass insulation with cement. All the kid did was get hopelessly entangled in glue.

We tried him on packaging next, but he couldn't keep count. Finally we made a porter out of him. I had quite a time convincing Bill's overly anxious mother that he wasn't ready to handle a more responsible job.

Harry's problem in a way was worse. A husky, middle-aged man, with a wife and child to support, he'd suffered severe back and leg injuries in an industrial accident. Even more serious were the psychological wounds he had acquired somewhere along the way. Harry was hopelessly neurotic. He had quit his last job because "everyone there was talking about me."

We hired him with some trepidation and assigned him to harness lacing. It didn't work. Harry needed a simple job, and he needed to work alone. The easy give and take of the bench made him frightened and hostile.

Fortunately, we had just the place for him. We put him off in one corner counting parts and inserting them in bags which he sealed by machine. As the jaws of the machine opened and closed, he opened and closed his own jaws in soundless rhythm. Those two "talked" to each other, and Harry was happy. His wife was happy, too, when he brought home a much-needed pay check.

A crazy way to run a shop? Maybe so. But the man was working, wasn't he?

CHAPTER FIVE

THE HALT LEAD THE BLIND

"Picture the face of a clock," Art was saying. "Now, starting at 12 o'clock, bring the lacing around to 6 o'clock, then tie it—like this."

Art was showing our first blind employee how to lace an airplane cable assembly. I stopped for a moment to watch and listen.

Patiently, searching for words to describe what you or I would grasp by seeing, Art led his pupil through an intricate series of loops and knots. The other man followed Art's hands with his own, memorizing as he traced the movements.

"Okay, I think you've got it," Art said. "Now, try the whole thing from the beginning."

57

Gene Zamora, fifty years old, and sightless since birth, took a deep breath. He reached toward a bench rack, touched it, then felt along the edge until he located a small compartment filled with wires. He took a wire, felt for another compartment where he plucked a second wire, repeated the process until his groping hand held seven wires. Arranging them in three layers, he entwined them with cord, and tied the knots.

When he had finished, he held up a cable assembly that would some day be part of an airplane in flight. It was hardly more difficult than weaving baskets—but how much more rewarding for all concerned!

Gene learned fast. He had a remarkable sense of touch, like so many of the blind, and a gift for intense concentration when feeling his way through a new situation. Bent over the bench, his fingers flying, he was soon doing quick and flawless work.

In the weeks that followed, we added several blind people to the crew. One of them, a 51-year-old grandmother named Dinah Craik, became our first woman employee. She had five per cent vision, which meant that usually she could avoid bumping into people she met on the street. Her husband was also blind; for years they had scraped out a meager living with first one working and then the other at seasonal and fill-in jobs.

Dinah introduced a new element into the lacing rhythm. Her hands moved not from bench to rack and back again, but from bench to rack to her well kept hair. Art spotted it as he was making his inspection rounds.

"What's this?" he asked.

"What's what? Oh, you mean the bobby pins. These wires slip sometimes when I'm picking them up, so I clip them with pins until I'm ready to tie."

We kidded Dinah about the woman's touch—and then added her reach-and-clip system to the routine. It was useful not just for the blind but for others who had problems in grasping.

Angelo Zangara, a young man who suffered from cerebral palsy, assisted the blind on the cable job. Alex served as eyes for the others; he prepared and assembled the wires so that the lacers could work by touch alone.

Sight was about the only physical asset Angelo could claim. He hobbled with a foot-dragging, spastic gait, his hands trembled constantly, sometimes his whole body shook with the effort it cost him to attach a lug to a wire. Even his voice was a rasping, ill-controlled bark. But he managed. He worked so zealously the first day that his hands at quitting time were raw and blistered from the lugging wrench.

"Your badge of honor," Art said, as he bandaged the blisters. Angelo wore it like a badge, too. He was prouder still when he acquired like the others a well-calloused palm.

Angelo fell once with a clatter of crutches while dragging a bundle of wires. People looked up briefly from nearby benches, then went on with their business, as blind Gene Zamora reached out with sure hands to put Angelo back on his feet.

How different the scene would have been in any "normal" shop. Well-meaning bystanders would have exclaimed over Angelo, pawed over him, forced him to lie down whether he needed to or not. Company officials almost certainly would have called a worried meeting afterwards. And Angelo, probably, would have been asked to leave. For his own good.

At Abilities, he was just a man who fell down and got up again with a little help.

The Abilities attitude might have struck an outsider as insensible—even cruel. I didn't pamper the workers, and they didn't pamper one another.

There was a revealing incident when a new employee, a partially paralyzed man, kept pestering one-armed Jim Rizzo for help. All day long, he asked Jim to bring him a wrench, cut him a wire, help him open a drawer. It stopped abruptly when Jim shot back with: "Whassa matter, you crippled or something? Open your own drawers."

Cruel? Not really. It can be far worse cruelty to help too much and in the wrong way.

I remember vividly one of my own experiences with misguided help. I was a child then, just starting to school, but already too keenly aware that I was not like the others. A well meaning, utterly thoughtless teacher feared that stronger children might trample me on the stairs, and so she forced me to enter and leave the building by trudging up and down the fire escape. I hated that teacher. I used to time my classroom entrances, slamming the fire escape door so that her papers blew in wild disarray, until she gave up finally and allowed me to use the stairs with the rest.

I remember, too, the time I fell into the hands of a benevolent stranger in the New York subway. I was a grown man by this time, but still dwarfed by stump legs, and I was pushing my way at belt buckle level through a jostling rush hour crowd. Suddenly a man reached down, seized my arm, and began to propel me through the jam. He half pulled, half carried me up a long flight of stairs and out of the station where he cheerfully deposited me on the wrong side of the street. His intentions were fine, of course; it just never occurred to him that a cripple might have his own ideas on where he was going or how he wanted to get there.

As harness making and then cable lacing settled into smooth routines, we took on some new operations. One of them was a mailing service for several Long Island firms.

Chester Haase, a truck driver before he was blinded by accident, was assigned to the mailing bench. Letters and envelopes had to be arranged for him in the proper piles, of course, but he was neat and fast at folding and stuffing. One day he asked if he could take some work home to do after hours.

"Sorry, Chet," I said, "but this one's on a tight budget. There's not much room in it for overtime."

Chester looked hurt. "I don't mean for extra money, Hank. Just for something to do. I sit alone most evenings listening to the radio. I get nervous when my hands are idle." I explained about the State Labor Regulations against homework and so, reluctantly, Chet left his envelopes at the shop.

Another new operation was model toy work for Bill Effinger, our neighbor next door. That was the job we'd figured on months before, when Abilities still consisted of one employee and a telephone. Now Effinger was ready with a rush order.

The toy was a model airplane that could be flown drone-plane fashion on short wave radio signals. Our task was to assemble the receivers and transmitters, tiny, delicate parts which had to stand up against the tough treatment toys receive. They had to be tuned in precisely right.

We pulled several of our best people off other assignments to set up a radio department in one corner of the now bustling garage. Horace Johnson was put in charge as supervisor. He had developed already into a young man who could handle not only himself but others as well. His crew included three polio patients, a blind man, a paraplegic, and a man badly scarred and smashed from an auto accident.

The radio team clicked from the start. Special jigs were devised so that tools could be held by paralyzed hands. Assignments were planned so that each person brought his best ability to bear. And some new abilities were developed as they worked out their problems.

Blind Henry Lowell became inspector for the crew. Henry had tinkered with ham radio for years. Now he rigged up an electric circuit, attached a dial system calibrated in Braille, and installed a buzzer. The apparatus converted visual data into electric impulses, and allowed him to hear the gauge and meter readings which had to be tested.

Henry was a tough inspector. When he pressed a button he got a buzz, or he didn't get one, and you couldn't argue with his findings. But the rejects were few. Soon a steady series of buzzes from the radio bench announced that another job was rolling on schedule.

We were beginning to learn a great secret of disabled labor. "Matching abilities," I called it. Complement one man's strength with another's weakness and you gain sometimes the productivity of three.

All over the shop were efficient, smooth working little groups in which one man saw, another heard, still another furnished the fingers. But sometimes in the rush of improvising, we slipped up.

There was the lip reading deaf mute who had a terrible time breaking in. After a few days I became concerned and checked with Nierenberg.

"Something's wrong here, Art. This man seemed like a good prospect, but he's not producing. Who's his supervisor?"

Art named the bench boss and instantly comprehension dawned on us both.

Our lip reading worker was going crazy trying to take instructions from a supervisor who stuttered.

Our most inventive employee was Jim Wadsworth. A colorful character, he had been a boat captain and deep-sea diver in Alaska before he came to us. A diving accident, followed by the dread "bends," had left him paralyzed from the waist down.

Jim's injury was such that he couldn't sit comfortably for long periods. He solved that by hooking up a window cleaner's belt which allowed him to swing from his bench. Then he began prowling the shop in his wheelchair at odd moments, making suggestions to others. Soon he was serving as our methods engineer. Years of fussing with short wave radio, diving equipment, and other gear on his various boats had given him a unique capacity for jigs and fixtures.

Jim found one harness maker plucking awkwardly at the wires with partially paralyzed fingers. He took an awl, bent one end to make a hook, and fitted a loose piece of copper tubing over the handle. Thus the wires could be picked up with the hook and tamped into the desired position by sliding the tubing up and down.

Another time he observed a paraplegic trying to solder plugs with one barely usable arm. The man moved his arm crab fashion, elbow braced against the bench, as he reached for plugs, soldering wire and hot irons. Jim transformed it into easy work. First he took a spool and rigged the soldering wire on what amounted to a small crane. Another crane-like attachment with swivel was improvised for the irons. An arm-rest platform and an ingenious holder for the plugs brought all of the tools and materials within inches of the worker's hand. He could solder plugs now almost literally by lifting a finger.

Jim's biggest value lay not in such devices, useful as they were, but in his whole approach to a job. Most people develop mental blocks about routine, familiar things; if they see a foot pedal machine they assume that it has to be operated with the feet. Jim would have it switched around in ten minutes so that it operated by hand lever if that were more convenient. He was the kind of guy who couldn't wash his hands without pausing a moment to wonder why the faucets turned counterclockwise instead of the other way around.

Like a lot of inventive, imaginative people, he was

also an unreconstructed individualist. He could be irascible when things went wrong. And he didn't like taking orders from Art, who was younger and less experienced in many ways. After one particularly hot argument with Art, he quit. A man in Jim's condition can't "stalk out," but he managed to convey that impression as he wheeled away, stiff-backed and angry.

I let him cool off for a couple of days, then dropped him a note. He didn't answer. A few days after that, I went to see him. I found him sitting alone in a dingy furnished room.

"What the hell are you doing?" I asked. "Counting your money?"

"I'm minding my own business. Why don't you mind yours?"

"Jim," I said, "we need you. And you need us. Come back to work."

It was the right approach. Our methods engineer returned the next morning.

The old garage by now was beginning to look like a plant.

Outside, we had laid down a curb-to-door blacktop driveway to facilitate wheelchair passage. Before that, the employees had to fight their way through inch-thick mud on rainy days.

We put up an Abilities sign—a detail I'd overlooked in the early, frantic struggle to survive. Visitors no longer poked their heads in the door with an "Is this it?" expression.

Inside, the once drab and grimy cement block walls were painted sea green. I had done that one weekend with the help of an obliging brother-in-law. My wife, Lucile, had added some smartly tailored draperies to frame the windows.

We had a shop cafeteria. Not much of a cafeteria, perhaps: the equipment consisted chiefly of a donated refrigerator. The employees contributed some odds and ends of kitchenware and a decrepit old hotplate. It took nearly an hour to bring the water to boil, but it served the purpose if you plugged it in early enough. The set-up provided coffee three times a day and enabled the shop gang to add hot soup, milk and simple desserts to their lunch-time sandwich fare. We set it all up on a small painted counter and extended a gay awning over it. It was soon dubbed "The smallest snack bar in American industry."

My office was now a 15 x 20 foot cubicle fenced off from the rest of the plant by a knee-high railing. It was dubbed inevitably, "the bull's corral." The furnishings included a highbacked old swivel chair and a handsome rolltop desk, both prized loans from our friends at Sperry Gyroscope. They were the desk and chair at which Elmer Sperry sat when he was founding his company.

Along with these luxuries, Abilities had acquired a one-woman office staff in the person of Florence Fiedelman. Attractive, poised, well-groomed she seemed, at first glance an imposter in a shop for the severely handicapped. When she walked, however, you noticed the limp. One leg had been amputated above the knee.

Florence had no job problems; she gave up a well-paying position to join Abilities because "this is something I can put my heart into." She proved a godsend. Florence reduced to well ordered files the jumbled, chaotic mass of old records which I had stuffed into drawers and boxes. She set up new payroll and bookkeeping systems, took care of long, tedious reports we had to file, presided with crisp efficiency over a dozen details of office routine.

One result of all this efficiency was to make me more aware than ever of our precarious position. Did I exult at whipping a tough assignment? Florence laid on my desk a prompt job statement which showed that we whipped it just in time to keep from losing our shirts. Did I grow expansive when we hired new men? There was Florence again, with the payroll updated.

Success itself had become a problem. In less than two months we had grown from one employee to twenty-three. We were grossing nearly $1,000 a week. But a job that turned sour, or even a slight delay in getting paid for a job, could put a dangerous strain on our bank account. The week that my new secretary joined us, in fact, I had a payroll of $656.50, and only $1,947 in the till. We needed a steady stream of new work just to survive.

One job hunting expedition led to an unexpected adventure. It started with a tip from Don Bryce, an old friend of mine, who was then New York advertising manager for Dictaphone Corporation.

"Our Bridgeport, Connecticut, plant is talking about something called printed circuits," Don told me. "It's a new wrinkle in the electronics line—wiring without wires, they call it—and they're all excited about the possibilities. Think you could handle it?"

"Never heard of it," I admitted, "but I'd like to give it a whirl. Abilities is getting pretty good at electronic work."

Don set up an appointment for me at Dictaphone's Bridgeport plant, and agreed to go with me when I made my pitch.

On the appointed day, it rained. Then poured. Arriving at Don's suburban home, I found him in the basement, pants legs rolled to the knees, bailing out his playroom. "A slight emergency," he called cheerfully. "Be with you in a minute."

At the other end of the playroom, Don's wife paused, bailing bucket in hand, to push back a soggy strand of hair. "It appears to be raining," she observed mildly. "Hadn't you boys better wait for a weather report?"

We couldn't wait—we were already behind schedule. We assured her that the weather had to get better since it could hardly get worse.

Get worse though it did. Fifteen minutes after taking
the road we had to turn on the headlights and slow to
crawling speed along a rain-lashed highway. The wind
snatched at us in violent gusts. Several times the car
nearly flooded as we forded small lakes which sprang
up. By the time we reached Stamford we knew we
would never make it by auto. We nursed the car to the
railroad station, and climbed soggily aboard the next
train for Bridgeport.

At Bridgeport the storm was still going strong. There
was another delay while we shouted for cabs. Finally
we got one. When we arrived at the Dictaphone building we found the office closing early. Most of the
employees had left or were leaving. A few executives
were still hurrying around. I cornered one.

"My name's Viscardi," I said, trying to look brisk
and businesslike in my dripping garments. "I have an
appointment here to talk about printed circuits."

"Appointment? Printed circuits? Good Lord, man,
don't you know there's a hurricane on?"

We were there, though, and they sat down to talk.
We must have made a good impression. Later on, we
got the contract.

In December we held our first leadmen's dinner. It
was to become a regular event.

A leadman in our system served as an assistant foreman. He was a pace setter on his bench, he helped to

train new employees, and sometimes he took charge of a particular job.

Four of the leadmen were old-timers as Abilities measured tenure. Horace Johnson, Jim Rizzo and Bill Graham of the original harness-making crew had all earned the promotion. So had inventive Jim Wadsworth. Three others were relatively newcomers. They were young men, in their late teens or just out of them, but matured by hardship beyond their years.

Leon Valeray was one of this group. His disability consisted of scars—terrible scars both physical and emotional. A childhood accident had left Leon's face a twisted, unsightly thing. Plastic surgery had helped, but only a little. Growing up like that, he had become withdrawn and hostile. He had a habit of ducking his head to one side as though he could not bear to be seen. At Abilities his embarrassment eased; he worked alongside people who thought a man merely ugly was lucky enough. He became a leader because pride wouldn't let him lag behind those who were more stricken than himself.

Frank Rieger had a nearly opposite background. Life for Frank had seemed all bright promise only a short time before. He was voted the most popular boy in his high school class, was engaged to marry the most popular girl. Then polio. He was severely paralyzed in both legs. But Frank had held on to the best part of his dream. He still had the girl; his success at Abilities meant that he could plan on marriage soon.

Ronnie LeMieux, another polio victim, completed the leadmen's list. Paralyzed in both arms, both legs, he couldn't lift his hands when he came to Abilities as a harness maker. He crawled his fingers up the lacing board, like a man climbing a wall, and dragged the wires into position one at a time. Later he was able to drag several wires at a trip; he kept at it until his clutching hand held eighteen wires. Still later he learned to do the fine, exacting work required for the model plane radios. And somewhere along the way Ronnie discovered himself. He was at first a hesitant, indecisive kid who threatened more than once to give up. He emerged as a self-reliant, very competent young man.

The leadmen's dinner, with Nierenberg and myself to round out the party, was held in the private dining room of a smart and expensive restaurant. Some of the men seemed shy at first, a bit out of the element which they knew and understood, but a couple of cocktails took care of that. By the time we leaned back for coffee and cigars, the talk had settled into the kind of easy camaraderie we shared at the shop.

"I won't spoil a good dinner with a bad speech," I told them. "But I want to say this. Abilities is set to go places now. You men can go with it. As far as you want. You're the start of my management team. I'm going to keep you informed on what I'm doing, and why, and what I plan to do next." I paused a moment for emphasis. "I hope you'll be just as frank with me. If you've got any questions, anything you want to say, this is as good a time as any."

"All right, Hank." Jim Wadsworth was stubbing out his smoke with a deliberative gesture. "I have a question."

I was not entirely surprised. When you solicit frank opinions from a man like Wadsworth, you are almost certain to be obliged.

"What I want to know," Wadsworth was saying, "is why we put up with those everlasting investigations from the rehabilitation people. They keep coming around, asking questions, inquiring into our private affairs. I don't like it, Hank. The people on my bench don't like it. It doesn't seem to go with the personal dignity you talk about."

"I'll second that," said a voice on my left. "They were around just yesterday with another questionnaire."

"Okay," I said. "Let's thrash this thing out. A lot of our workers are referred to us by the state rehabilitation office. We teach jobless, disabled people new skills and get back part of the training expense in return. It's not a special deal for Abilities; all industry is encouraged to do the same.

"As to the questionnaires," I continued, "you may be taking personal offense at a purely routine bit of government business. But I know how you feel; I'm the same kind of guy. I don't like that part of it either."

"Then why do we go along with it, Hank?" Wadsworth was still pressing his point.

"Truthfully, Jim, because we can use the money."

"Hank." It was Bill Graham now. "How much do we get out of this deal?"

"Offhand, I couldn't say precisely. It came to probably three thousand dollars for the first three months."

There was a long pause. It was a lot of money, for Abilities, and they all knew it.

Graham re-phrased the question: "What would happen if we didn't get that money? Would we go broke?"

"Certainly not!" I said. "But it would make a difference—a big difference. We'd have to tighten up. I couldn't give raises as fast. . . . "

"We can wait for our raises." It was Wadsworth again. "Let's do it, Hank. Let's run things our own way."

I glanced around the table, saw the heads of my leadmen nodding assent. Shop boss Nierenberg wore a bland, imperturbable expression, but the corner of one lip was twitching with what threatened to be a wicked smile.

"All right, boys," I said. "You want it. You've got it. If things get tough, remember that you asked for it." I wheeled around, making a small production out of signalling for the check, as I tried to hide the sudden warm rush of pride I felt for these tough and scrappy men. I knew the Division of Vocational Rehabilitation people would understand and stand by for when we needed them.

Going home that night, I reflected wryly that the

leadmen's dinner had been expensive beyond all calculations. Still, I couldn't bring myself to regret the impulsive decision.

It was a debt I owed. To Abilities.

By Christmas we had 41 people. Abilities celebrated by giving a party for employees, their families and friends of the company.

It was like all plant parties, which is to say that it developed along lines only slightly related to the original plan.

The shop Santa was a one-armed Irishman who showed up about two hours behind everyone else, and about six drinks ahead. There was a general rush forward of mothers when this jovial but unsteady St. Nick began tossing children into the air. We managed finally to calm the mothers, retrieve the children, and divert Santa with the suggestion of a drink in the men's room.

A buffet dinner was followed with music. We had engaged a Harlem trio, but somehow they failed to appear. Johnny Schmidt, of Abilities, a man with a broken back, substituted valiantly and well on a rented piano. People sang, a few danced. Our ebullient Santa returned to the action, whirling Florence Fiedelman through an old-fashioned waltz to the delight of everyone except possibly Florence herself.

In short, cheerful chaos. Eventually all hands departed with fat Christmas turkeys stuffed under their arms. I was just locking the plant door when three figures loomed out of the darkness.

It was the Harlem trio, complete with saxophone, accordion and drums. They had taken the wrong bus, wandered all over Long Island, and searched for hours to find the garage. They were stranded now, miles away from what they described as civilization, and they seemed to think that it was mostly my fault.

Well, it was Christmas Eve. I loaded the disconsolate trio into the car and drove them back to New York. Then, gratefully, I headed for home. When I arrived, Christmas Eve was giving way to Christmas Morn. My own youngsters had long since been tucked into bed— fat, rosy Nina, elfin Donna and baby Lydia. I promised myself that one of these times I would forget Abilities for at least a few days and get re-acquainted with my family.

I slumped exhausted into an overstuffed chair and watched Lucile and Nana tie the final ornaments on the tree. But forgetting Abilities was hard to do. As I watched the shimmering ornaments my mind's eye reverted to the shop party and I saw the faces of Wadsworth, Nierenberg, LeMieux and the rest. I fell asleep in the chair.

The next day was a quiet island surrounded by fragrant odors from the kitchen and the happy sounds which children make when they open presents. It was a merry Christmas.

CHAPTER SIX

WE LEARN THE HARD WAY

"A new wrinkle in electronic equipment," my friend Don Bryce had said when he tipped me off to printed circuit work at Dictaphone Corporation. I discovered that Don was understating the case. Printed circuits were so new that even the contractor didn't know the exact details of how to make them.

In theory, it was simple. Brilliantly simple. Some genius had discovered that he could print a copper etching on a board, add solder, and make that circuit substitute for a maze of conventional wiring.

In practice, however, it was at that time hardly more than a laboratory trick. Several hard problems had to be worked out before it could be mass produced for industrial use.

A dozen big laboratories were working on it. A dozen big laboratories—and now one little shop in a converted garage. Dictaphone Corporation had given Abilities a crack at one of the pioneer production jobs.

I was thrilled at the vote of confidence which this contract implied. I could hardly wait to report the good news to my advisory board. But the board, to put it mildly, did not share my enthusiasm.

Board chairman Preston Bassett leaned back in his chair and arched his fingertips in a reflective gesture as I made my report. When I had finished, he gently shook his head.

"It's too new, Hank. Too experimental. You can run into trouble on this one."

"Don't touch it, my boy," Director Raymond Jahn said flatly. "This is one contract you'd better refuse."

Refuse? After going through a hurricane to get the job?

"Don't let the shop gang hear you," I said. "They've got it more than half licked already."

The reply was rhetorical; the shop, in fact, was just beginning to dig into the problem. I was optimistic, though, because Jim Wadsworth was doing the digging. He usually found what he was looking for. Assisting Jim was Wally Pacceroni, a methods engineer on loan from Dictaphone. The two worked side by side, consulting at every step, so that we wouldn't waste time on experiments which Dictaphone had tried and discarded.

The basic unit over which these two men labored was a little waxed board, about four inches wide and six inches long. Laid out on the board was the printed circuit—a copper track which looped and twisted in convoluted design.

Fourteen component parts—resistors, condensers, capacitors—had to be plugged into a single track. They were tiny parts, the largest being about one-fourth the size of a cigarette, and they were attached to the board with bits of fine wire. It amounted to a hand stapling operation. Then one side of the board was dipped into a solder bath.

The solder presented the principal problem. If it was too hot it melted the copper circuit from the board. If it was too cold it formed lumps or didn't adhere to the track. And the results varied with split-second changes in timing. Jim and Wally tried quick dipping at high temperatures. Then slow dipping at lower temperatures. They fussed endlessly over the bubbling cauldron of solder, making minute changes in what they called "the brew." After much tinkering, they came up with a dip that would do the job.

There remained the special adjustments required for Abilities people. Here the problem centered around plugging in the component parts. The attaching wires were about the size of fine sewing thread and they had to be inserted in holes tailored to provide a tight fit. Our workers, many of them with crippled hands, couldn't manage the wires if they had to hold the boards.

Wadsworth fixed that easily by rigging a small pneumatic clamp. It locked or unlocked with the touch of a button and held the boards steady while wiring progressed. Like many of our special devices it proved so useful that it became a routine tool whether a handicap was involved or not. Later, Jim improved on it with an ingenious holder which could handle eight boards at a time.

Stanley Pilarski, a paraplegic, took the job from there. He broke the project down into four basic tasks, trained teams for each assignment, and set up an assembly line. Component parts were plugged in at the first stop on the bench. Tag ends of the attaching wires were clipped at the second stop, bent over and locked into place at the third. At the end of the line, a man with tongs reached for a board, dipped it for a five-second solder bath, then reached in quick rhythm for another board.

After that, it was just hard work. We completed a trial order of two hundred printed circuits and got a reorder for two thousand more. We did so well on it that we were able to cut our price per unit from $1.43 to $1.29. We shaved the price twice more in the next six months. We've been making printed circuits ever since.

I'm afraid that my advisory board had to put up with a pretty triumphant Viscardi when next we met.

My pride, unfortunately, was the kind that goes before the fall. I was sure now that Abilities could do anything, and in my confidence I plunged into situations where more experienced operators moved cautiously or not at all. Sometimes by luck and nerve and sheer effort we brought it off. But sometimes we got hurt.

One unhappy experience was a slip ring assembly job for Ford Instrument Company. It proved at least as tough as printed circuits and, while it wasn't quite as experimental, it might just as well have been. It was brand new to us.

A slip ring is a critical component used in motors. A tiny bullet-shaped affair, molded with plastic powder, it is cast in a hollow die under tremendous heat and 5,000 pounds of pressure. The die is cooled, then cracked open with another press to extract the bullet. Finally, three small platinum rings are attached with protruding wires.

Leadman Frank Reiger spent several days at the Ford plant, learning the process and getting checked out on the equipment we would use. Meantime, Nierenberg and I decided that we'd better take a quick course in die casting technique. We paid flying visits one day to several molding houses in Brooklyn and Long Island City.

It snowed heavily that day, and I went skidding around back streets of the industrial districts on my artificial legs, pushing Art ahead of me in his wheelchair. I discovered before our tour was half done that the going was likely to be slippery on our contract, too.

"You've got that job?" one man asked with a slight lift of the eyebrows when I explained the reason for our visit. "Well, good luck to you." He seemed to think we would need the luck.

"I wouldn't touch it," another assured me. I found that several molding companies had backed away from the job.

Okay, so we had another bear by the tail. We were bear tamers, and it didn't occur to me that this time we might get bit.

When Frank Rieger returned from his inspection trip he reported that slip rings at Ford were still in the trial and error stage. The die cracking equipment, for instance, consisted of hand-pumped hydraulic presses designed for laboratory use rather than mass production. The set-up in general was pretty primitive. But Rieger thought we could handle it. He took charge of a small crew and started to work.

Assigned to the job was Tiny Olafson. Tiny weighed more than 400 pounds, a condition due partly to illness, and he was twisted into almost pretzel shape by rheumatoid arthritis of the neck and spine. Shuffling through the plant, bent nearly double, his head twisted stiffly to one side, he looked a very awkward giant. In fact, however, he was surprisingly adept; he had been an athlete and musician in happier days.

Tiny worked from a big oak chair reinforced with steel. A special bench was sawed down to a height convenient for his enforced crouch. He cracked open the completed dies by leaning his huge, misshapen body against the handle of the press. Then he reached in with those surprisingly skillful sausage-shaped fingers and gently extracted the bullet-shaped part.

Another crew member was Bill Wiggam. Head injury had produced what amounted to a short circuit in Bill's nervous system. His brain was not affected but messages from his brain often failed to reach his hands. He dropped almost everything he picked up. He had control enough to pump a press handle, but that was about all he could do.

We made him a press operator for polio-paralyzed Rieger, joining his strength to Rieger's skill with hands. As Bill pumped, Rieger swiftly inserted, removed and disassembled dies. Bill, though, didn't like doing just half the job. At lunchtime and other odd moments, he practiced picking up small objects, trying patiently to improve his finger control.

Bill's practice sessions were painful to see. He would place thumb and forefinger over a die and pluck at it with intense concentration for minutes at a time. Once in a while he managed to bring it up to eye level and return it to the bench without letting it slip. And slowly, with great effort, his performance improved. One day, very proud, a die tightly squeezed in his fingers as the visible evidence of his hard won success, he reported to my desk.

"I've got this thing licked," he said. "I'd like to run my own press."

We talked Ford out of another press and Bill was content. It left Rieger with a problem—he wasn't strong enough to handle the pressing part of the operation—but Wadsworth fixed that by rigging a hydraulic hand valve with reciprocating air cylinders. The result was a much faster press which required almost no manual effort.

Nierenberg added a final touch. Dies hot from the molding were dunked in a water bath and we had to change the water at frequent intervals to keep it cold. Art hooked the bath into the plant plumbing system so that the water change became constant and automatic.

During all of this time we took a financial beating on the job. That was expected; we often lost money while learning how to handle a new operation. Now, finally, we had this one set up. The men were trained, the methods worked out. By endless experiments we had cut production time in half. We were getting quality. We were ready to roll.

But we didn't roll. We got rolled over. The Ford people who were most friendly to us, got a change in orders from their customer. Regretfully they cancelled our contract.

My friends on the advisory board were sympathetic but not surprised. "If you're going to gamble," Preston Bassett reminded me, "you must be prepared to lose at least half of the time."

He was right, of course. But we hadn't built our shop

on the principle of play-it-safe. When another opportunity arose, optimistic Viscardi was ready to gamble again.

This time it was an order for winding solenoid coils. Another new operation for Abilities people. The coils, essentially, were hollow plastic bobbins wrapped around with hundreds of layers of fine contact wires. The wires had to be wound tightly and evenly, tied off with special knots, and soldered at terminal points with a precision beyond anything we had done before.

It was a top secret job, during the Korean War, and we weren't told what the coils were for. I had a strong hunch that they were timing mechanisms for an extremely important piece of military hardware.

I knew—indeed, I was not allowed to forget—that they were wanted fast.

The contractor provided a winding machine and sent an instructor to get us started. Art set up a high speed production line and picked Harold Miller to supervise the job. The polio which crippled Harold had spared his hands, and he had received special training in jewelry manufacturing. Precision was his specialty.

Little dark-eyed Margaret Timmons, deformed of spine and legs from polio, was assigned the exacting job of tying off the solenoids. Eugene Melanesi, crippled in an accident, and William Cohen, a paraplegic from wartime injuries, soldered the terminals. They were able to turn out twenty solenoid coils a day.

The contractor said it was not enough. Almost daily we got anguished pleas to hurry, hurry, hurry.

We couldn't increase production without another winding machine. The contractor couldn't supply one. I had been warned against tying up too much capital in equipment, but this seemed an exception. So, I bought the machine. Art hired four new workers to form a second team and we got production up to forty coils a day. It still wasn't enough; the contractor now asked for fifty a day.

I called the eight workers together and put it up to them. Could each team step up production by five coils a day and still maintain the quality?

They could, and did. Sometimes they had to stay until eight or nine o'clock at night to do it, but they never left the shop until they had their quota of fifty coils.

Suddenly, in June, we began to get rejects. We couldn't understand it. We were testing every coil, and I was certain that only perfect coils were being sent out. The inspectors at the other end were just as certain that the work was defective. In desperation, I called E. U. Da Parma, the Sperry executive who had given me my first real briefing on the electronic business.

"Uly," I said, "we're in a coil winding jam, and the worst of it is, we can't find out what we're doing wrong." I outlined the problem.

"You need an expert," Da Parma said. "I'll send one over."

Uly sent Fred Narveson, a quiet, thoughtful, almost professorial man, and one of Sperry's top trouble shooters on coils. Fred went through production and testing procedures with us step by step.

"It looks all right," he admitted, then added: "But, obviously, there's a problem somewhere. They don't send these things back for fun."

He puttered around in seemingly aimless fashion, rechecking a point here and a point there. He wandered over to the wall, looked at a thermometer we had tacked up, and stood for a moment tapping the bowl of his pipe against the palm of one hand.

"You know," he said, "these coils are full of funny little bugs. You take temperature, for instance. You test a coil here, at your temperature, and then check it somewhere else under slightly different conditions, and you don't necessarily get the same result. You've got a pretty hot little shop here; that might be throwing your test readings off. If that's not it, I'll come back for another look."

He didn't need to come back. When we adjusted inspection for a difference in temperature, we were back on the track.

And then, without notice, someone in Washington decided that these particular solenoid coils weren't so urgent after all. The old Army game of "Hurry up, and wait." Or maybe a coil directive got lost in the Pentagon. Anyway, Washington cancelled our contractor's order. He cancelled ours.

It cost us a staggering $1,200.

A few weeks later we got burned again on an assembly job for an airplane company. This time the assignment looked easy, and it should have been easy, but we got a little careless.

The job was to rivet four parts together to form a gun trough. When we put the parts in a vise, however, they didn't quite fit. I called a foreman at the contracting company for instructions.

"File them off until they do fit," he said.

We filed our way through four hundred parts and the company rejected every one. We had to re-do them at a heavy loss. It didn't help any when I found that the foreman had given me the wrong advice. I was furious—at him, partly, but mostly at myself for not making sure.

I consoled myself with the dubious theory that bad luck runs in threes, and turned with relief to a more familiar kind of work. An electronic cable job this time, for Grumman Aircraft. We had done cable assembly before and, while this one was a little different, we were back at least on well-known ground.

I was especially anxious to do well at it because we had a fine friend and good customer in David Rittenhouse, who was in charge of Grumman's manufacturing division. A famous ex-Navy pilot—he's still called "Commander" though he's long since hung up the uniform—Dave took a personal interest in Abilities. He toured our plant and invited me to show a film on disabled workers at Grumman's plant. He had given us a dozen small orders, and he was moving us steadily up to more important assignments.

The cable work went well—at first. Our men quickly picked up the minor variations required for Grumman, then settled into smooth production stride. We had been shipping for six weeks when Rittenhouse called me.

"Hank," he said, "you're in serious trouble on these cables. Better get over here."

I couldn't imagine what was up, and I didn't want to go unprepared. I called in the boys—Art, Jim Rizzo, who was our top on cables, and Frank Rieger, who was in direct contact on the Grumman job. They couldn't offer any suggestions; in fact, they were convinced that our people had been doing the job according to the instructions received.

I left a worried crew behind me as I streaked off to Grumman. I was worried, too, and became more so when I saw Rittenhouse. He is a tall, solid man, erect and disciplined. His lean, taut face is usually impassive —but today he looked absolutely sick. He had placed a great deal of faith in our little shop, and apparently we had let him down hard.

Several Grumman men gathered in the office—Joe Jeransky, the foreman, Johnny Mason, an inspector, and Ben Gambe, head of inspection. For 45 minutes they piled up the evidence that the cables we had made were inferior in every conceivable way. "This is a bad solder joint." "This lug is loose." "This tie is loose."

Gambe ended his summation with, "on this basis we cannot continue to send this work to Abilities, Inc."

Just like that, a job involving 2,400 man hours of labor went to pieces before my eyes.

I was stunned. I could make no defense, offer no challenge to any of their statements. So I sat and took it. But when Gambe finished his justifiable criticism I bounced back enough to say, "I don't understand why your inspection department was so slow in rejecting these cables. Why didn't they tell us the first day that they were no good? Why did they let us ship for six weeks?"

The Commander revived, too, at that, and repeated my question to his men. They had no answer.

"Give these cables back to us," I pleaded, "and send someone to show us *exactly* how you want them made. We will correct them."

"When shall we send them?" Rittenhouse asked.

"Now!" I replied, "I will take them with me."

The fault had been ours; the Grumman people had placed too much confidence in us. Now, with the Commander's hand in it, we got a top-notch training supervisor. We buckled into it, determined to salvage what we could from the worst fiasco of all.

Ronnie LeMieux reorganized the operation. Ten men had worked on the original job, each man making an entire cable from start to finish. This time we did it assembly line fashion with a team assigned to each of three stages. The first team stripped the ends of the cables and inserted them into the plugs. Another team soldered the wires in place, while a third crew attached the vinyl covering and capped the plugs.

Ronnie was up and down the line, checking the work at every stage, to spot imperfections before they showed up in the finished cables. That saved a lot of waste effort. He also made time studies and set the teams to competing against one another.

We worked as even Abilities had never worked before. Our reputation was at stake. Our bank balance, too. Our very survival. Those spoiled cables had become a rope around our neck, and we fought like the devil to get it off.

The big try was exemplified by Joe Rado. Joe was polio crippled and shy and desperately anxious to please. We put him on cables without specifically saying that he was no longer to work at his old model radio assignment, and not knowing which job had priority he tried to do both. He asked to work overtime. So it was that Art spotted him one night busily repairing cables on top of the bench and ducking under the bench to work on model radios when the flow of cables slowed for even a moment.

With people like that going for you, it's hard to lose. We got the rope off our neck. We came out of it, in fact, with a big order for more cables.

When the cable mess was straightened out, I took time out to sit down and think. I could blame some of our disasters on bad luck, some on circumstances beyond our control. But we were making too many mistakes. Half a dozen times recently, rejected work had cost us money we couldn't afford to lose. Our customers were rightfully critical. After all, we had set the ground rules: a better product at a better price delivered on time.

I thought I knew the answer, but I wanted to talk it over with someone who could view the whole thing in a detached, objective light. Someone who really knew the business. I placed a phone call to Da Parma at Sperry.

"Uly," I said, "it's Hank. A long time ago in an empty garage you gave me the first lesson in how to operate an electronic shop. I think I'm ready for the second lesson."

That evening we met for a long talk. I gave him the whole story. When I had finished, he made a wry grimace.

"You boys must be in an awful hurry, Hank. It sounds like you're trying to crowd all of your mistakes into a couple of months." He shrugged, eloquently dismissing irretrievable errors. "You know what to do now, don't you?"

"I think so," I said. "Our main problem is rejects. We'll have to get better inspection in the shop."

"Right." Da Parma leaned forward, ticking one forefinger against the other for emphasis. "There are two big things to remember about inspection, Hank, and the first one is this:

"Double check your first piece of work on every job. Make your contractor test it; get his verdict in writing. Don't turn a screw on the second piece until you know absolutely that the first piece is right.

"Secondly, you need in-line inspection. Test every stage of a multi-stage operation, not just the final piece. You're doing that on the cables now. You ought to do it on every job."

I thought of the man hours we'd lost, the thousands of dollars, because Viscardi had jumped into a tough league without knowing these simple rules. But then, if I had received this advice earlier, perhaps I wouldn't have realized how much it was worth.

"One more thing, Hank." Uly grinned to take the sting out of the words. "Remember that quality is built into a product, not inspected into it."

We set up an inspection department with Horace Johnson in charge and assigned polio paralytic Milton Goodman as his assistant. Milton was such a confirmed perfectionist that he always fell behind on bench work; now we turned to advantage his almost fantastic insistence that everything be done just right.

We tore our production system apart and set it up new. We had grown in hasty, sprawling, unplanned fashion, adding a bench here and a bench there for every new job. As a result, we had bits and pieces of related work going on helter-skelter all over the place. Now we broke the jobs down to simple components, organizing the benches to do specific tasks of wiring, soldering, assembly and the like, without regard to the particular contract involved. It proved more efficient.

We made foremen and department heads out of our best leadmen and helped them to take night school courses. We passed a rule, too, that every employee had to be checked out on at least three different operations. That gave us more flexibility in planning our work. Our front office saw some changes, too. The shop was getting too big to be run out of Viscardi's hat. I drew more people into the office staff, gave them more responsibility.

One of the best of the new office people was Sam Abrams, retired from the cloak and suit business, who became the first head of our purchasing department. Sam was over 65. He had high blood pressure, a poor heart, a weak back, hernia, and an incurable zest for life and work. He was to die one day on his way to work. I think he wanted to go out that way.

Sam was the toughest bargainer I ever knew. At Abilities, he got stuck only once on a purchase—a case of paper cups which proved defective—and he raised so much hell about it that the salesman sent over two free cases and told us to keep the original case, too. Whereupon economical Sam issued a shop ukase that the leaky cups would have to be used first. The cafeteria floor was drip-stained for weeks.

The boys got even with Sam a little later when he bought some prosthetic urinals for the paraplegics. "Look out for quality, Sam," they said. "Remember the leaky cups!"

So ended our first season of discontent—with little jokes about little mistakes we could afford to make. We didn't forget, though, the lessons learned by big mistakes.

If reminder was needed, there was a little copper-wired coil on Viscardi's desk. A reject, salvaged from an expensive job that had gone all wrong. I used it as a paper weight, but its real function was to serve as The Symbol.

When I called a conference of department heads, and the boys found me flipping The Symbol from hand to hand, it was understood that sloppy work would be freely discussed.

CHAPTER SEVEN

SOME HUMAN DIVIDENDS

"One of these days, Hank, they're going to back an ambulance corps up to the door and haul at least half of these people away."

It was Dr. Sidney Glasser, our part-time plant physician. We were having a familiar argument.

Dr. Glasser was a warm-hearted, fatherly, rather cautious man, and while he applauded what we were trying to do, there were times when the details scared him.

The doctor was shocked when he found an epileptic in the plant. "Hank," he said, "that man may keel over without warning at any time. He might injure himself."

"He may keel over," I replied, "but not without warning. He tells me that he can feel a seizure coming minutes in advance. He leaves the bench and sits down quietly somewhere and has his fit. He's in no more danger here than he would be any place else.

"Besides," I added, "the guy's nineteen years old. What do you want me to do, Doc? Send him home to sit by a window for the rest of his life?"

One day Dr. Glasser laid on my desk a medical survey on the hazards of hiring disabled workers. More than half of the nation's plant physicians, the survey showed, thought it unwise or unsafe to hire a heart patient. Two-thirds of the physicians would reject the blind and amputees, four-fifths would turn down paraplegics, epileptics or those suffering from cerebral palsy. More than 90 per cent wouldn't pass a worker suffering from active rheumatoid arthritis. We had people in all of those categories—and some with problems even worse.

The survey was new and so were the statistics. But it was the same old story I'd heard so often before.

"This interests me," I told Dr. Glasser, "even more than you know. Abilities is in business to prove that this whole damned blacklist is absolutely wrong."

We shared our physician's concern for the health and safety of our people. I was convinced, though, that tradition-bound personnel managers and company doctors had overestimated the danger of accidents. The disabled man is a careful man; he knows the consequences of a slip. Our plant safety record was almost twice as good as the average industry.

I was convinced, too, that from a health standpoint alone the inevitable hazards were more than balanced by the good medicine of active, useful life. I could find examples all over the plant.

Ronnie LeMieux, for instance, crawling that paralyzed hand up the harness board, dragging a wire, and improving in weeks until he could drag eighteen wires. Physical therapists would call that an exciting gain.

Or huge, arthritis-twisted Tiny Olafson. He'd slimmed down from more than 400 pounds to less than 300 since he came to work. Maybe it was an illusion, but I thought Tiny walked just a little straighter now.

Bill Wiggam, too. Controlling his fingers, forcing himself to pick things up, when by all rules he wasn't able to do it.

We had people who quit stuttering at Abilities, and a deaf and dumb man who started talking, and a paralytic who came in thrilled one morning to report that he had wiggled his little finger for the first time in ten years. Work seemed a wonder drug for many ills of both body and mind.

But Dr. Glasser warned me not to expect too much:

"When a human nerve cell or muscle has been destroyed, Hank, all the exercise in the world won't bring it back. It's like an electric fuse—when it blows, it's gone."

"Maybe so," I admitted. "You're probably right. But maybe, sometimes, it's like a dead battery that can be recharged."

Someday, I promised myself, we would look into this question. We had planned from the first that Abilities would become a national center for rehabilitation, for medical research. And what a fascinating human laboratory the shop would make! We might find out at least a little of what goes on inside a person when you give him a reason to live.

We didn't have the facilities for it now, or the money, or the time and energy to spare from our daily struggle. All that would come as a reward for success. Meantime, I didn't have to wait to learn how we were affecting our people in their daily lives. I could see them change in appearance, in personality, in self-reliance and skill. I could swivel around in my old leather chair and look out over the shop and count the human dividends we were declaring every day.

Sam Carson was a case in point. He established a record of sorts by winning the first fist fight at Abilities.

I had to pretend annoyance when it happened, but I was secretly a little pleased. Taking a good, hard poke at someone or something was what Sam had needed to do for a long time.

Sam was a deaf mute. How much was physical, how

much psychological, I never knew. I did know his background, and it explained a lot. He came from a family
that was poor in almost every respect—in money, in
education, in love and understanding for their difficult
child. His father once threatened to kill him with a
butcher knife.

He had spent a good part of his childhood and most
of his adult life in institutions. When he came to Abilities, he was confused and resentful, slow to understand
and difficult to instruct.

Sam, in fact, had developed his defect as his one defense against the world. When he didn't want to
understand, he couldn't.

We gave him a job to do, and let him alone, and he
got by. Not a top hand by any means, but he tried.
During a bus strike, he walked more than eight miles
to work one morning.

Then we hired another deaf mute, and it developed
that the two were old acquaintances, though hardly
friends. The second man was a bully; he found a natural
patsy in Sam when they were in deaf mute school together and he took up now where he had left off. Time
and again he goaded Sam with soundless finger-waving
harangues. Sam would stand and take it, or sometimes
just walk away. And then, one fine morning, Sam
turned on his tormentor.

It was a one-punch, one knockdown fight. I didn't
see it, but I was informed that for a man who hadn't

done much swinging in life, Sam mustered a pretty convincing right to the jaw.

Nierenberg suspended both men in the interest of shop discipline, but Sam took refuge in his special defense. He couldn't understand. Art wrote it out. Sam, bent over his work bench now, very busy tinning wires, pushed the note aside. He had no time for correspondence.

We let him stay. The other man didn't come back when his suspension was up, and we were just as happy to see him go.

Sam's fistic prowess enlivened cafeteria conversation for days. But that was as nothing compared to his second sensation. Art Nierenberg brought me the news one morning, an odd excitement shining in his eyes.

"Hank! Sam's talking!"

He was, too. Not much, just three words. He had taught himself to mumble, "Good morning, boss."

John Ederly got his job by mistake.

John was on our waiting list, and when we needed another man for our fast growing packaging department we called him in. His application showed that he was paralyzed in his right wrist, hand and leg following surgery to remove a brain tumor when he was eleven years old. Just out of high school, he had never been employed. "A mine-run cripple," as we say at Abilities. We hired him.

I didn't know at the time that John was also an epileptic. If I had known, I probably would have let Dr. Glasser talk me out of this one. Though I never admitted it to Doc, I, too, was afraid at first of this problem.

John didn't try to hide his epilepsy. He noted it dutifully on the second sheet of his application, under Medical Remarks, but fortunately for him that sheet got lost in another file. Those were the days before Florence Fiedelman applied her orderly instincts to our magpie nest of a filing system.

So John got his job. He did fine for about three months. Then one day he trembled, stiffened and went into a rigid, almost death-like trance. It lasted thirty minutes. Afterwards, he insisted that he was all right.

Nierenberg and I held a worried conference. "Art," I said, "some day we'll have a full time nurse, a decent medical room, a lot of facilities for emergency treatment. Maybe then we could handle him. But now—I don't think we can risk it."

Art agreed, but I could see that he hated to fire the man. "I'll tell him myself," I said. "Send him in to me."

John appealed the verdict. He pointed out that his seizures were but short episodes compared to long intervals in which he was not affected. I shook my head brusquely; it was a painful interview and I didn't want to draw it out. John persisted.

"I've been here three months," he said. "I've had one fit that cost thirty minutes of work time. That figures out to what? About thirty seconds a day, average, isn't it? I'm a good worker. I more than make it up."

He had me, and he knew it.

"Okay, John. You win. But next time, leave the bench when you feel it coming on. We'll fix up a place where you can pass out without getting hurt." As I waved him away and went back to my paper work, I reflected wryly that Viscardi was losing his grip. I was now getting lectures on disabled efficiency from a nineteen-year-old kid.

In the months that followed, there was less and less need to worry about John. His attacks became less frequent, less violent. Sometimes he would go six months or more without a perceptible seizure. I asked him about it once and he told me that he could control it better because he felt more secure.

"Everybody here knows I'm an epileptic," he said. "And nobody cares. That helps a lot. I'm not all tensed up about it anymore. If I feel it coming, why, I just relax and have it."

It remains a small point of pride with him that sometimes he can "have it" so imperceptibly that someone sitting next to him will not be aware. There was, for instance, a shop cafeteria incident when he felt the familiar symptoms while enjoying his morning coffee and roll. He braced himself gently, folded his arms, and waited for the seizure. It quickly came and went. John had a hard roll in his hands and as his fingers turned rigid the roll crunched noisily, then shot from his grip.

"Dammit, Art," John said to Nierenberg afterwards, "I think I could have slipped by with that one. But I forgot to put down that damned roll."

Emmett Hood was another who stretched even our standards of ability.

Cancer had eaten away Emmett's larynx, leaving him unable to speak in the normal fashion. In a desperate effort at repair the doctors cut a hole in his throat. He "talked" through that hole, training a new set of muscles to force the words out. It sounded like a series of liquid gurgles, but by dint of great effort he could make himself understood.

The illness cost Emmett the job he had held for twenty years. He had seven children to support. And the doctors questioned that he had six months to live.

For Emmett there seemed no hope. I started to reject him, then something tugged at my memory.

"Haven't you been here before?"

"Yes." He labored to form the words. "I applied here three months ago."

Three months! A long time for any man to pound the streets in search of work. To a man who carried his burdens it must have seemed forever.

We gave him a job.

Then he really got lucky. The cancer which had been spreading so long apparently quit spreading after a final operation. The brief time allotted to him came and went and he still lived. Triumphantly and incredibly, he lived.

When Emmett joined us he signed on as a temporary worker. As such, he did not receive the life insurance policy we provide for regular employees. About a year later he buttonholed Doc Glasser and reopened the question.

"I think I'll be around awhile," he said in that strange voice of his. "I'd like a permanent job."

He got the permanent job, and the life insurance policy that went with it. For Emmett, it was a kind of certificate of survival.

The success with Emmett encouraged us to hire others who suffered from cancer. The almost miraculous recovery was not repeated, but another kind of triumph emerged.

There was Paul Kargis who was riddled with cancer and knew he was dying. His bladder had been removed; further treatment could only postpone for awhile the sentence he faced. At the edge of death, however, he still clung to two ambitions of life. He wanted to hang on long enough to see his first grandchild born. And he wanted to pay his debts.

Paul was an accountant by trade. By nature he was withdrawn and stoic. For months he worked in our bookkeeping department, doing his work well at whatever cost of pain and effort, keeping coolly aloof from those about him. Meticulously he informed Art of the time he would be absent for treatment; aside from that no word of his illness ever passed from his lips. Then gradually he began to change. He was a reserved man still, but in his own quiet way he became warm, almost mellow.

He achieved his two ambitions. The day came when he had to leave us.

"Working here, being part of Abilities, has changed my whole outlook on life," Paul told Art at parting. "I've seen what other people have to endure and how they endure it. I'm not afraid anymore of what will happen to me."

When Murray Nemser applied he was carried in. On a litter.

"I have to score you A for effort," I told him. "But how can you work? How can you even get to work?"

He lay there and looked at me, his eyes begging me to grant him a trial.

Murray had been a handsome, vigorous young fellow once, six feet tall, 195 pounds, a successful salesman.

Then war. A shellburst in France all but tore him apart. His feet became frostbitten, osteomyelitis set in, in both legs. Other complications followed. When he was brought home his wife and parents could not recognize the sixty-pound skeleton he had become.

A brilliant doctor moved heaven and earth to save him. Bone grafts, skin grafts, operations without number. In the process his hips, knees and ankles were fused so that he could no longer either sit or stand. He could only lie on a litter-type wheelchair, his shoulders slightly elevated. He seemed doomed to a vegetable existence for the rest of his days.

Murray didn't need a paycheck particularly; his military pension allowed him to provide for his wife and two children. But he desperately needed something to do. All day long he lay at home watching television until he knew every program by heart and hated them all. He ran out of conversational subjects and felt so left out by life that to talk seemed pointless. He felt, as he told me once, like a dead man whom someone had forgotten to bury.

He tried to get a newsstand concession but the deal fell through. Then he heard of Abilities. His wife and brother-in-law loaded him, litter and all, into a car and brought him to our door.

"How can you get to work?" I asked him again, and he jerked his head in the direction of the car outside.

"Like I got here today. I can work if you'll just put the tools in my hands."

Murray's mechanical problems actually were solved with surprising ease. He came and went stretched out in the back seat of a taxicab. He needed only a little help from the driver to ease himself from seat to litter at each end of the trip. At the shop Art rigged a lacing board above his chest so that he could work in the prone position.

He thrived. Soon he was leadman for a crew of five. He went on to a still more responsible front office job.

He became expansive and confident. People who called at his home now had to compete conversationally with a man who had plenty of things to talk about. Murray will really bend your ear if you give him an opener like, "How are things at the shop?"

The daily ride between his home and his work is a long one and the cab fare takes a pretty big bite out of his paycheck. Murray doesn't mind. Money is only the least of many things he's working for.

Alex Alazraki's misfortune occurred before he was born. At some point in the mysterious process which forms a new life, something went wrong. He entered the world without arms or legs.

Arm stumps which ended above the elbows and leg stumps chopped off above the knees were all that saved

Alex from being a basket case. What saved him from sitting out his life, in a basket or anywhere else, was his own indomitable courage.

Alex developed in the rounded tips of his arm stumps a tactile sensitivity that was incredible to see. He could dress himself, button his shirt, tie his necktie, comb his hair and shave. He could control a pencil with those amazing stump-end muscles and write clearly. In high school, he volunteered as a secretary to gym teachers because he loved to be close to sports.

His parents wanted to protect him and provide for him. Alex wanted to provide for himself. When he came of age, he was chagrined and embarrassed because his mother still tried to help him dress. He fled the parental home for a rented room in Brooklyn, his native city, and took a job selling newspapers at a subway exit. It was all he could get.

The newsie business in Brooklyn is a pretty tough racket, but Alex by now was a pretty tough boy. He sold papers twelve and fourteen hours a day in all kinds of weather and he survived and flourished. Then they rebuilt the subway in a way that spoiled his location. With no more customers coming up out of the dark, noisy caverns, his newsstand concession wasn't worth a dime.

Alex didn't mind too much; he was ambitious for better things. He invested most of his life's savings in a car, sank the rest of what he had in a stock of fluorescent lights, and set out to be a traveling salesman. And that nearly ruined him. The lights didn't sell. The people he met away from his familiar neighborhood stared at him as though he had escaped from a cage. He went broke. When he came to us, at 34, he was still scrappy, still defiant, but the fear showed through. His voice betrayed him with a shrill, unnatural squeak.

He said he could handle packaging. I doubted it.

"Try me," he said, the words confident, if the tone was not.

We sat him down to a packaging job where he had to count out fifty little screws, put them in a bag, and seal it. Almost immediately he was working rings around Helen Pearson, a polio paralytic, who sat next to him on the bench. It caused an emotional scene. She went home in tears at being beaten by a packer who had no hands.

But people got used to being beaten by Alex. They had to. He came the day after Christmas, and in less than six months he was bossing a crew.

Blonde, blue-eyed Helen Pearson was in her late twenties when she came to Abilities. It was probably the first important decision she had ever made.

Helen was paralyzed by polio early in childhood, and for many years after that she existed in a protected island provided by parental love. She grew up without ever having had a date, or a dollar of money that was really her own. She was the kind of girl who cried easily when beaten at picking up screws.

Under the soft surface, though, there was steel in Helen. She displayed it when she came to Abilities over the heartfelt protest of parents who did not understand her need to work. Having made that decision, she found it easier to make others. She wanted a car, and her parents thought she was not able to drive, and she got the car.

The car opened up rich new possibilities of life. Helen came and went now as Helen pleased, not at the convenience, or inconvenience, of someone else. She began to go on picnics and outings with other disabled women who worked at the shop.

Helen Pearson, Mary Meredith, Frances Kelley—polios all—formed a close-knit little circle of friends at most of the outings. Then, after a while, it became a little less Helen, Mary and Frances, and a little more Helen and David Wilson.

David worked at Abilities, too. A shy man, in his early forties, he had a background like Helen's in many ways. His heart had been dangerously weakened in childhood by rheumatic fever. He, too, had led a sheltered existence for most of his life.

It was a quiet courtship but there was never much doubt about how it would turn out. Three years after they met, they were married. They joined a growing new-married set in the shop.

Seven months later, David died. At life's end, he had crowded in more of life than he had ever known before.

Esther Caldwell might be accounted by some not a success story at all. It depends on what you call success.

Esther was born blind. She was able to absorb that first blow, however. She had a fine mind, and a strong will, and she found a compensation for blindness in the inner light which comes from ideas. She struggled hard for an education, achieved a master's degree in sociology. Then, unaccountably, her body failed her again. She became deaf.

The double disability made it impossible for her to continue in her chosen work. She had to contend, moreover, with a third, man-made kind of handicap. Esther was a Negro. It was a savage irony that she was barred from many places by a color difference which she had never seen.

An ordinary thing like househunting was a nightmare for Esther. Even deaf and blind she had no difficulty in sensing the rejections; she could feel the doors closing in her face. During one bitter period she groped for weeks through a strange city seeking just a decent room in which to live.

When she went job hunting she found nothing—nothing at all. For five years she eked out a thin existence on public relief. Living alone, cut off from all contact with things that give meaning to life, she withdrew more and more into the dark, soundless prison of her tortured thoughts. Finally, in desperation, she wrote to someone who might be able to help and have the heart to care.

"I don't want to live off the taxpayers," Esther wrote. "I want to be one. I want to make some use of the only life I will ever have. Surely there must be someone, somewhere, who will give me a chance. . . . "

She addressed it to Mrs. Eleanor Roosevelt.

Mrs. Roosevelt gets hundreds of letters from troubled people, and she answers them all. It is one of the traits of character which mark her as a great lady. She put Esther in touch with us.

Our only immediate opening was a job in the packaging department. Esther took it. It was not, of course, the happiest solution for a university graduate; it was just far better than no solution at all. Later she became a harness maker.

The physical problems were quickly worked out. We used a braille machine to instruct her at first, then switched to the simpler method of printing with a finger on the palm of her hand. Often she would sense the word when it was half spelled, and grow impatient.

"Yes, yes," she'd say, nodding abruptly or wiggling her thumb. You develop a kind of shorthand if you talk often with Esther.

Not so easy were the personal adjustments which

Esther had to make. The years of misery and rejection had hurt her deeply, and some of the scars were slow to heal. It was evident in many ways.

She hitchhiked to work every morning—not from economic need, but from some inner compulsion to test herself daily against the unseen, unheard dangers of an alien world.

She withdrew sometimes into brooding silence. She would come in, take her place at the bench, work all day and depart with only a stiff nod to acknowledge the presence of others. A day or two might pass like that; then a quiet "Good morning" from Esther would announce that she was emerging from her private torment.

Sometimes when her mood was darkest she would sit on the packaging line, taping cardboard boxes, and as every hundredth box passed beneath her hands, she would tear it to shreds. But if she was not "adjusted," she was fighting hard—and that in itself is a form of victory. We counted an occasional torn box a small loss.

I wish we could have reached out and touched her and healed her and made her whole. All we could give her was a small bit of dignity in the form of a job. Perhaps in time that would help her find peace.

CHAPTER EIGHT

WORD GETS AROUND

People like to hear success stories. As Abilities grew and prospered, I found myself talking to groups all over the country.

Once, bone tired at the end of an exhausting week, I caught a midnight plane to address a business convention at Miami. I arrived at dawn, reached my hotel in time for a shower and breakfast, squeezed in an hour's nap before I was due to go on. From somewhere I summoned the energy to put the speech across.

Afterward a man came up to be introduced. I felt rewarded for the hard journey when I heard his name. He was the head of a large company, a firm which Abilities had been trying to crack for months.

"An inspiring story," he said, taking my hand. "Truly inspiring. You are doing a wonderful thing."

I thanked him, then added quickly that we hoped to get work from his company.

"You'll get it," he promised. "This kind of effort deserves support." He suggested that I direct a letter to his attention.

I went home elated and wrote the letter at once. When he didn't answer, I dispatched a second letter. This time I received a polite, evasive acknowledgment signed by a minor official of the firm.

"I have been asked to look into this matter. . . . I regret to say that there seems to be no immediate prospect. . . . Please be assured of our continuing interest. . . ."

It was, unmistakably, the brush-off.

Perhaps the man who made the promise meant to keep it. Maybe he was so surrounded by assistants and executive secretaries, so hedged in by corporate procedure and union rules, that his good intentions never filtered down through his organization. That happens in some big companies. Or, maybe, when he got back to his comfortable office, the problem of disabled people didn't seem so urgent after all. That happens, too.

The reasons didn't matter. It was, to us, just the old, familiar story of faith without works.

Disgusted, I crossed off that lead and vowed for the hundredth time that I would quit shouting a message which no one really wanted to hear. But within a week I was on another plane, to Atlanta, Georgia, this time, to participate in a medical conference on rehabilitation.

A few days later I received a letter from A. P. Jarrell, a Georgia health official who had been a prime mover in arranging the conference. It seemed a routine thank-you note, and I started to scan it hastily before tossing it aside. Then one paragraph caught my eye.

"An outstanding industrial surgeon called after the conference," wrote Jarrell, "a man who examines the job applicants for six business firms. He said that this meeting has given him a new insight into the whole question of disabled workers. He's going to press for a complete change of policy in the companies he serves."

So it wasn't all waste effort. One man had heard; he was willing to act. Because of that, the hard struggle might become a little easier for dozens of injured, abandoned people.

This was part of the answer for the girl who wrote that Abilities had not reached her where she sat in her wheelchair on a porch in Kansas. Perhaps one day Abilities would be everywhere. Meanwhile we might reach out into the hearts and minds of men and change some lives. There were so many that needed changing.

I sat creasing the letter, thinking of the people who might be helped; thinking with sudden awe that I was planting seeds which might blossom some day for men and women whom I would never know. Then I bowed my head in a little prayer of contrition and thanks.

About this time I received an honor which wasn't intended for Viscardi at all. It happened like this:

A distinguished citizen award was to be made by the Junior Order of United American Mechanics, a fraternal and patriotic organization which has long since lost its mechanical connection. The award includes a scroll, a gold medal, and $5,000 in cash. Bernard Baruch was selected for the prize.

Baruch declined with thanks, and graciously suggested me instead. "Mr. Viscardi deserves it," he told the donors. "His company, Abilities, Inc., is the most important event in the U.S.A. this year."

The nominating committee had considered me, but Baruch was their choice. They stuck with it. Baruch was equally insistent that I should get the award. Finally the elder statesman arranged a compromise.

"Viscardi has collected his share of scrolls and medals," he told them, "and I've got a pretty good collection of money. So give him the $5,000, and I'll accept the honor."

The organization quickly agreed, and so, of course, did Viscardi. Who was I to argue with a Baruch plan?

The money was especially welcome, as I was now badly in need of new housing for my growing family. Even more welcome in a way was the chance to meet and speak to this body of more than 2,000 first rank business and professional men. These were people who hired other people. They were the kind of audience I most wanted to reach.

And so, when I received my slightly second-hand award, I tried once again to paint the vision that burned within me. The vision of a proud, free country which would allow all of its people to share in the freedom and pride. "Neither pensions, parades nor pity," I told them, "can compensate for the sweet dignity of productive life."

When the meeting broke up, Baruch took me aside to mix praise for the speech with a gentle scolding. "You ought to make more talks like that, Hank. You ought to go up and down the country, telling every businessman in America."

I reflected wryly on my seemingly endless round of planes, trains, hotel rooms and platform rosters. Already tucked in my wallet was a train ticket for the next convention.

"I'm on the circuit," I assured him. "Sometimes I think I'm going around for the second time."

A few weeks later we received a surprise visit from Baruch. He called from a nearby Long Island gun club one day, and said that he'd like to see the plant if I could send someone over to guide him.

"Wonderful," I said. "You're not far from us now. I'll pick you up in about ten minutes."

I jumped in the company car with Danny Gibbons,

our one-armed "over-aged" chauffeur and handyman, and we wheeled through traffic with the nonchalant ease which is Danny's forte. At the gun club, I transferred to Baruch's station wagon while Danny led the way back.

Wearing his familiar panama hat, Baruch leaned back in the well cushioned seat and looked at me quizzically from under his bushy white eyebrows.

"Hank," he said, "I was at a dinner party the other night and someone there was very critical of you and your operation."

I didn't know what to say, so I said nothing. He waited awhile, then asked, "Well, aren't you going to ask me who he was and what he said?"

"No, sir," I answered. "I feel that if you want to tell me, you will."

He laughed and slapped his knee. "In my long years of experience, Hank, I've found that's one way to avoid criticism. Don't ask for it."

We dismissed the critics then, and talked of the belief we shared in what I was trying to do. Baruch, I knew, was in my corner. He had written the introduction to my first book, *A Man's Stature*, and had given staunch support to my work at J.O.B. The rehabilitation effort behind J.O.B., in fact, was largely financed by the Baruch Committee on Physical Medicine, which he set up in memory of his father, a pioneer surgeon.

"My father started this whole concept of physical

rehabilitation," he told me once. "Before he died I promised that I'd carry it on."

Baruch inspected the plant for more than an hour,
asking shrewd questions, and not bothering to conceal
his own disability as he held out his famous hearing aid
to catch the answers. Tall and erect in his conservative
gray suit, he maintained his habitual composure throughout, but there were tears in his eyes when he turned
to go.

"Hank," he said, "I'm overwhelmed."

We put his visit down as a surprise birthday present.
It came just a year and a day after we opened the shop.

What with one thing and another—work mostly—
we didn't get around to a birthday party until nearly
two months after the event.

We scheduled our party for the Georgian Room of
the Garden City Hotel. That was for sentimental reasons. I had attended a lot of harried luncheon conferences in the Georgian Room, had bolted down a lot of
ill-digested meals there, during the worried days when
I was trying to raise a few thousand dollars to launch
our great adventure. It seemed a fitting place for a banquet of triumph.

The day of the banquet was perversely foul. A blus-
tery nor'easter came whipping in from the Atlantic,
soaking Long Island as only a seaside locality can be

soaked. I was dictating a final letter in my office, before leaving for the party, when the phone rang. It was a hotel official, wanting to know if we intended to keep the reservation.

"Sure. Why not?"

"Well, uh, I mean, your people. . . ."

He was a nice guy who didn't know any better, and I laughed at him.

"Mister," I said, "you underestimate our people. They have survived war, disease, mistakes of nature and disastrous accidents of every kind. You name it, they've had it. Did you think a little rain was going to spoil their party?"

The storm, in fact, didn't even slow the party down.

At the hotel, someone found an old wooden ramp and laid it over the outside stairs. It was wet and slippery within five minutes, but no matter. The people who had to use it knew how to manage. They came sloshing out of the rain and struggled up the ramp as though it were some special kind of red carpet in their honor.

Inside, Dr. Glasser bustled around dispensing warm handshakes and worried looks as he urged new arrivals to get out of their wet coats right away. I thought that some of Doc's handshakes seemed unusually protracted. Nierenberg caught it, too, and pulled me aside with a confidential grin.

"Hank, do you know what I think?"

"No, what?"

"I think Doc's taking pulses on the sly."

We both laughed. When Doc fussed over us, or at us, we knew it was an expression of love.

The banquet room was noisy and crowded. Milling around the long table were more than 250 people: our employees, their wives or husbands, and the friends of Abilities.

Jim Wadsworth and Sperry's Uly Da Parma sat heads together in earnest conversation in one corner of the room, solving an engineering problem, no doubt. I made a mental bet that they would be scrawling designs on the tablecloth before soup was served.

Charlie Langdon was present, collecting a well-earned steak dinner for all those cartons of coffee he brought when Nierenberg sat alone in an empty shop.

Preston Bassett was there, too. Just returned from Europe, he had chartered a private plane at Halifax in order to arrive in time for our celebration.

There were many others whom we could be proud to call friends. People who had loaned us money, trusted us with important jobs, helped us in a dozen ways. I had to get them all together in one room before I realized how much we owed to their wholehearted support.

After the dinner we settled back over coffee and cigars and listened to the pleasant sounds of praise. Arthur Roth was one of the principal speakers. A banker, accustomed to dealing in facts and figures, he outlined the Abilities story in its stark statistics.

In a year's time we had created new jobs for 57 men and women—all of them people who were "unemployable" by almost any standards but ours.

We had sold $191,526.65 worth of goods to nine different firms.

Despite the trial-and-error hazards of learning new jobs, training new workers, we had emerged with a first-year profit of $48,090. We had paid back our investors in full, had laid by reserve funds to safeguard Abilities against slack times.

We were giving steady raises—our employees were earning an average of 29 per cent above their starting wage—and we were providing other benefits like medical insurance and paid vacations.

Roth cited the statistics of success, then paid tribute to the workers who made it possible. "Not the least of your abilities," he told them, "is the great reservoir of spiritual force which you have brought to the task."

Bassett spoke also, his quiet, almost shy sincerity adding impact to his words. "Abilities," he said, "has been a surprise to us all. We on the advisory board have learned much more than we taught. No hale and hearty man could have imagined the things that you have done."

When it was my turn I rose and looked out over my tough and gallant little crew, and knew that I didn't have words enough for what was in my heart. So I made it short.

"We don't have a dais for honored guests," I told them, "because we couldn't build one big enough. All of you belong on it."

Mrs. Eleanor Roosevelt was another good friend of Abilities who paid us a visit. By pre-arrangement, I picked her up in New York City one day for the drive to the plant. Almost at once, she asked about Esther Caldwell, the young woman she had referred to us.

"Esther is having a hard time," I said. "A very hard time. But she's trying hard, too. I think she's going to be all right." I told her of Esther's lonely struggle.

As we left city traffic behind and motored through the wintry Long Island landscape, I reminisced with Mrs. Roosevelt about other meetings and other times. I remembered, especially, the first time we met, during World War II.

I was a brash young man then, full of fervent ideas about how to help war amputees, and I had just been fired from the Red Cross for trying to do too much too soon without going through channels. Mrs. Roosevelt heard of it, and summoned me to the White House. Gently, with great tact and charm, she drew out my beliefs on what ought to be done. She encouraged me to continue my efforts on another front.

"When you are ready," she said then, "let me know. I think perhaps I can help."

It was, I discovered, no idle promise. I was invited back for another long talk in the pleasant garden of her Hyde Park home. I was put in touch with men who could do something about jobs for the disabled—men like the CIO's James Carey, and General Electric's Charles Wilson, who was then head of the War Production Board. I wound up touring war plants to plead the cause of disabled workers.

At one plant I arranged to "disguise" myself as a regular employee. I worked in the tool crib for awhile, was transferred to the foundry department, did paint spraying and other jobs. Then I sat in at a plant conference on hiring the disabled.

"Hank, here," the plant superintendent nodded toward me, "has been making a special study to determine whether any of our jobs can be handled by disabled veterans." He turned to one of the supervisors. "What would your reaction be to trying an amputee in your department?"

The man shook his head. "Wouldn't work."

"Why not?"

"We've got a tough schedule to meet. We don't have time to fool around with a one-armed or one-legged man. Hank has worked in my department; he ought to know that."

The superintendent grinned. "You reported that Hank did a more than satisfactory job. It may surprise you to learn that he's a no-legged man. He wears artificial limbs."

"Well, I'll be damned." The objector swiveled around to give me an astonished look. "I noticed you limping a little, but I didn't think. . . ." He paused, embarrassed, then stuck out his hand. "Seeing's believing. I guess I've been wrong about this."

Thanks to the support of Mrs. Roosevelt and others, I was able to put on several such demonstrations. Industry's walls of prejudice didn't come tumbling down, but cracks began to appear in the walls. A few factories started to hire disabled men.

Later, when I was offered the post at J.O.B., Lucile and I went to Hyde Park to talk it over with Mrs. Roosevelt. Again, she reinforced my convictions with her own great faith in the limitless possibilities of human beings. Due partly to her urging, I threw away a secure future in private business to gamble on a new idea.

Still later, when Abilities began, there was a good luck message from Mrs. Roosevelt on opening day. Her letter and one from Bernard Baruch hung for a long time on our bulletin board, two proud adornments of an otherwise almost barren shop.

Now I was taking my guest to see the fruit of a long labor. As we swung into the Abilities drive, I tried to keep a poker face.

"It's just a garage," I said. "But I think we're doing some pretty good work."

Our guest was expected, but even so a quick ripple of excitement went through the plant when she stepped through the door. Heads bobbed up from work benches.

People poked their neighbors. Other heads bobbed up. The shop rhythm slackened and hushed for a long moment, then the rhythm resumed as busy hands returned to their tasks.

Mrs. Roosevelt didn't know it, but Abilities had paid its highest compliment. Our people don't often stop work to watch a visitor come in.

Moving up and down the line, pausing often for friendly chats, Mrs. Roosevelt toured the shop. She lingered longest when she was introduced to Esther. You could sense the warm greeting without hearing the words as the older woman printed her message into the young woman's hand.

Someone took their picture together so that Esther would have a souvenir, though she could not see it.

Blind Gene Zamora was thrilled when Mrs. Roosevelt stopped to inspect the work he was doing. He started to extend a hand, retrieved it quickly to wipe it on the bib of his overalls, then extended it again. "It's an honor to meet you," he said.

"No," she said, taking his hand, "it is my honor."

Our guest lingered also with Alex Alazraki, marveling at how he packaged tiny rivets with his handless stumps. I told her that Alex hoped to have surgery so that his leg stumps could be fitted to artificial limbs.

"Godspeed, Mr. Alazraki," she cried.

"I want to come up in the world," he wisecracked, "like the boss."

Afterward, Mrs. Roosevelt told me, "Hank, this is wonderful. I had no idea that you were accomplishing so much."

"It's only the beginning," I said. It was a promise, not a boast.

Midway into our second year, the National Association of Manufacturers asked me to speak at its annual meeting. I jumped at the chance. Here were the top people in industry, the very top. At one stroke—by a simple change in attitude—they could take a long step toward wiping out the unspoken and unspeakable policy which consigns millions of our citizens to the national scrap heap.

A few days after I wired my acceptance, a brisk, competent looking fellow paid a call at my office. He introduced himself as Byron Keith, representing NAM.

"Mr. Viscardi," he said, "we've been thinking about your spot on the program. Instead of the usual routine— the formal introduction and so on—we'd like to open with a dramatic presentation of the problem."

"Dramatic presentation?" I said. "Mr. Keith, to convince this audience I would dance on a tightwire to demonstrate disabled agility."

He laughed. "That won't be necessary. But I think we've come up with something that will be pretty effective."

The plan was to build a short play around an episode from my autobiography, *A Man's Stature*. The acting, Keith told me, would be handled by professionals. At an appropriate moment, I had merely to rise from the audience and launch into my talk.

It sounded good, and I liked it still better when I saw the script. The incident they planned to dramatize dealt with my Red Cross experience, in World War II, but it went to the heart of the problem for all disabled people in peace or war.

On convention night I sat in the Grand Ballroom of New York's Waldorf-Astoria and had the odd experience of seeing myself walk across a stage. The actor who portrayed me was good; I noticed with a start of recognition that he had picked up little mannerisms I hardly knew I had. I nodded with professional approval at the way he handled his "artificial" limbs. He limped a little, but not too much, as a man would if he were used to walking on aluminum legs.

My attention shifted to another actor, at the far side of the stage. Huddled in a hospital bed, eyes turned toward the wall, he portrayed a young soldier named Jerry.

Jerry—the real Jerry—was a soldier who never got past training camp. He was climbing into the back of a G.I. truck one day when another truck caught and pinned him from behind. He lost both legs.

When they brought him to Walter Reed Hospital,

where I worked, Jerry was still in emotional shock. He had been able to endure the gangrene, the stump surgery, the months of traction, the endless pain. What he couldn't endure was the thought that his injury was somehow a mark of disgrace and failure. He couldn't bear going back to his small town and facing his family and friends.

"I didn't even lose my legs in a shooting war," he complained the first time we met. "I'm half a man and not that much of a hero."

I pulled up a chair and offered a cigarette. "Don't worry about missing the war, soldier. You're going to be fighting another kind of war for the rest of your life. You'll have a chance to prove you're a man."

In the months that followed, I coaxed him, kidded him, bullied him when I thought it would help. He began to bounce back. But one day I found him withdrawn and bitter. He waved me away; he didn't want to talk about it. I sat, and waited, and finally it came out. An old leg maker in the prosthetic appliance shop had looked at Jerry's stumps and pronounced them too shattered to support artificial limbs. He wanted to make Jerry a small cart, close to the ground, so that he could propel himself with his hands.

"That's all I need," Jerry said. "Then they can give me a cup and some pencils and I'll be set for life." He turned his face away, but he could not stifle the sound of a sob.

I talked to his doctor. "You're not going to let them put Jerry on a cart, are you?"

"No, the leg maker was a fool to tell him that. I think something can be worked out."

After still more surgery, Jerry got his limbs. I taught him to use them. We practiced walking—on gravel paths, over curbs, up steps and down ramps, on rough terrain and smooth until he knew instinctively how to balance himself and make new muscles substitute for those he no longer had. He drove himself like an athlete in training. The time came when he could no longer put off thinking about going home.

"What am I going to do, Hank? I'm scared. I can't face the people at home. You've seen my family's letters —there's a broken heart in every paragraph."

"They'll have to learn to live with it, Jerry. As you have. I'll talk with them if you think it will help."

And so I went to Jerry's little town in Pennsylvania. I found there elaborate preparations for his return. The civic organizations were going to parade him down Main Street. The mayor was going to appoint him town tax collector. An easy job at a nominal salary; enough to keep him in pocket money as he spent his days in a chair in the sun.

Late into the night, I talked with Jerry's parents. It was hard to tell these well-meaning people that the homecoming plans were terribly wrong. When I had them convinced, there was still the rest of the community.

The mayor had done more than anyone else to organize the affair, and he resented my intrusion. We had a long argument.

"Mayor," I said finally, "why don't you just stick this boy up on the courthouse lawn. Like a used cannon."

Shocked and angry, he jumped up from his chair.

"You have no right to say that. We're trying to do what we can for Jerry. We're trying to take care of him."

"Mayor," I said, "suppose it wasn't Jerry who lost his legs. Suppose it was you. Would you want to be taken care of? Would you settle for what you're offering him?"

He sat down again, the white anger draining slowly from his face. "I hadn't thought of it like that before. I guess you're right. I wouldn't settle for that."

Once persuaded, the mayor went all the way. He helped me to rent a motion picture theater, the town's only place of public assembly, so that I could talk to the entire community.

At this point the dramatization ended, and I rose in the Waldorf ballroom to give once more the talk I had made long ago in a drafty, threadbare little Pennsylvania theater. Memories and emotions came rushing back as I told of Jerry's long struggle to walk upright again, of his desire to go home like any soldier returned from the war and take his place as a man among men.

I went on to speak for the nameless millions who shared Jerry's hardship—and his need. I pleaded with these captains of industry and dispensers of jobs not to doom the disabled to idleness and despair. "Give us," I begged, "that one big break—a chance to work, to be self-supporting, to enjoy the full rights and obligations of citizens."

"We will earn our paychecks," I promised, "and you don't have to take my word for it. Come to Abilities and see for yourselves what the disabled can do."

When I finished, 5,000 industrialists rose and applauded. How many of them went back to their plants and rewrote their employment policies, I never knew. But the speech did some good at least; the NAM launched a study of disabled employment and asked me to take part.

It was another small crack in the formidable wall.

Still another event was turned to Abilities advantage. It came about thus:

I was a member of President Eisenhower's Committee on Employment of the Physically Handicapped and was scheduled to receive that organization's distinguished service certificate. What interested me a great deal more than the certificate was the fact that the principal speaker for the occasion would be Ralph J. Cordiner, president of General Electric Company.

I had been trying for a long time to get a GE contract. With no luck. Maybe this was my chance.

I was allotted ten minutes for my part in the presentation program and I began to scheme and connive as to how I could use that brief interval to create a dramatic impression. I came up with an answer but I wasn't sure I had the nerve to do it.

I still wasn't sure when I stood on the dais and received my certificate. As the master of ceremonies went through the presentation routine I stole a glance at Cordiner. He looked formidable. Not the kind of man you'd want to put on the spot.

Then I was on and I had to make up my mind. I decided to go through with it.

"I appreciate this honor very much," I said. "But I'm not going to make a speech about it. I'm waiting like the rest of you to hear Mr. Cordiner's speech."

I turned and looked directly at him. "I'm going to do you a little favor, Mr. Cordiner, and warm up your audience by telling a story. Then I'm going to ask you to do a favor for me."

I turned back to the rest of the audience, slid into a story I often use for convention purposes.

"You've heard a great deal today about my artificial legs. The problem is not as profound as you might think. After all, it's a question of alternatives. When you go to bed you take off your shoes and socks. I don't. I just take off my legs.

"The other day my wife looked at the socks I was wearing.

" 'Hank,' she said, and something in her tone of voice should have alerted me. 'Hank, are you wearing argyles again? Don't you ever wear plain colors any more?'

" 'Sure, honey,' I replied, 'but you laid 'em out for me.'

" 'Darling,' she persisted, 'the last time I laid out any socks for you was the day before the baby was born.' Her voice rose. 'Hank Viscardi,' she practically shouted at me, 'haven't you changed your socks for nine weeks?' "

I waited for the chuckle and got it. A quick side glance at Cordiner. Was that smile merely polite?

"Despite the compensations," I continued, "there can be unforeseen difficulties with artificial legs, as I recently discovered when I made my first overnight trip in a roomette. I don't often travel by train. Being pressed for time, I usually go by plane. But this time my secretary—who is an excellent secretary despite being disabled—happened to notice the sky was threatening and the wind rising. She was afraid LaGuardia Field might be weathered in by morning. So she cancelled my flight and reserved a roomette for me.

"The word sounded pleasantly romantic. I had never been in a roomette before. I found myself descending to the cavernous regions of Penn Station and traversing the long platform with agreeable anticipation. A room of my own—a roomette—a nice, quiet, cozy place in which to go over my notes for next day before turning in for the good night's sleep I pretty much needed.

"It was cozy, all right. But I must not get ahead of my story.

"Before he left me, the porter said, 'Just turn this handle, boss, and the bed'll come down out of this wall panel and you hook it over there.'

" 'Okay,' I said, without paying much attention, and plunged into work on my notes. An hour or so later, I decided I had better get some rest.

"I turned the handle the porter had indicated and this Murphy attachment started to descend upon me. Before I knew it, I was right through the open door into the outer aisle. When the bed stopped, I stepped back inside. It took some squeezing to get my rather husky frame into the scant ten inches of space remaining. Then I looked around for the spot on which I was to latch the contraption. I found the hook, of all places, on top of what my children call the johnny seat.

" 'Fortunately,' I thought, 'my plumbing is okay, if my legs are not. I won't have to unearth this johnny seat in the middle of the night.'

"The space was so narrow I couldn't sit on the edge of the bed, as I do at home, to unfasten my legs. I had to sprawl full length on my downy couch with my artificial appendages extended straight out in front of me. It took some twinges and some grunting, but I finally managed to unfasten the various straps and buckles.

"I shoved the sixteen pounds of paraphernalia—metal,

rubber and leather—intact with footgear—overboard into the little remaining space. There wasn't an inch to spare. My rigging filled it completely. But at least I didn't have to sleep with the machinery.

"Well, I had what you could broadly call a good night's rest. The next morning the horns of my dilemma closed in on me again. How was I, in the name of all the dimensions, including the fourth, to get up off this darn shelf, slam the contrivance back up into the wall, get my two legs back on again, and then get those recalcitrant limbs into my trousers? Which one of these four operations should I undertake first?

" 'Well, Hank,' I said to myself, 'disabled people are supposed to have magnificent compensating ingenuity. Now you use it.'

"I took what there is of Viscardi without the legs and deposited him in the wash basin. Then I reached over and released the traveling bed. In doing this the tender portions of my anatomy hit the tap that turned on the hot water in the wash basin. There was the darndest yell you ever heard. I catapulted off the wash basin and successfully dodged the rising bed only to find myself entangled with those two legs, maliciously lying in ambush, it seemed, for just this opportunity. I really have just *two* artificial legs, but, at that moment, with all those straps and buckles wrapping around my neck, I felt I was dealing with an octopus.

"In the midst of my struggle for survival, there came

a commanding rap on the door. It was the porter. 'What's going on in there?'

" 'It's all right,' I called back, 'the three of us will get straightened out in a little while.'

" 'Are there *three* of you in there?' he demanded.

" 'You can go away,' I said, 'we'll be okay.'

"Well, I finally unravelled the situation. Some time later, after I had shaved and dressed, I went out in the corridor to disembark at the Union Station in Washington. My porter was waiting for me. As he took my bag, he gave me a knowing look. 'Man, I've been railroading twenty-seven years,' he said, 'but this is the first time I ever knew of anyone having *two* women in a roomette.' "

I got the laughs I expected as I went through the story and a good long laugh at the final punchline. Now I braced myself to deliver the real punch.

"All right, Mr. Cordiner," I said. "I've done you a favor and warmed up your audience. Now I'm going to ask a favor from you. I'd like you to warm things up for Abilities by giving us some work."

There was a sudden hush in the hall.

I had been brash, probably rude, but I didn't care. Not if it worked. I only worried about how Cordiner would take it.

His first words reassured me.

"Mr. Viscardi," he said, smiling broadly, "you've made yourself a deal."

GE's mills, like those of the gods, grind slowly sometimes and many months passed before the deal was
finally nailed down. But nailed down it was. We had a
new customer.

President Eisenhower's Committee on Employment
of the Handicapped scheduled a three-day exposition in
Washington, and Abilities decided to show its wares.

No doubt our booth annoyed some people because
we flaunted the fact that we worked for money.
"OPEN COMPETITION, NOT SHELTERED
WORKSHOP," we proclaimed defiantly on one huge
sign, and on another, "A BIG NEW HAND FOR
PRODUCTION." Our posters revealed people hard at
work at useful, important tasks; our shelves displayed
what such labor could produce. In the booth, to show
how it was done, were Nierenberg and Alazraki.

Baruch spent a day at our booth, showing us off in
proud godfather fashion. Vice President Nixon paid the
booth a visit, then Mrs. Nixon came with Mrs. Eisenhower; soon the First Lady returned with the President
himself. Mr. Eisenhower picked up our theme of "Ability, Not Disability" and made it the theme of his key-
note speech to the exposition. Nearly two hundred
congressmen and senators also viewed our display. The
Washington newspapers said we stole the show.

Unfortunately, there were some who regarded it as

just a show. Along with the people whom we wanted
to reach, we had to put up with a stream of idly curious
who, it seemed, came merely to gawk.

One overly curious woman proved particularly an-
noying. She all but pawed over Alazraki as she harassed
him with questions that became ever more personal.
Finally she asked him if he could dress himself.

He told her he could.

She wanted to see him button his shirt.

Alex is a gentleman and so he merely stared through
her, and past her and went on lacing cables with the
rounded ends of his agile arm stumps. He felt like
throwing her out of the booth.

The gawkers stung me more than I knew. The
memory of it was still strong months later when Nierenberg appeared in my office one morning to say we'd
just received an invitation from another exposition, in
Chicago.

"We're not going," I snapped. The decision was
formed as I spoke the words.

Art spread his hands in a placating gesture. "A few
people in Washington made you sore, Hank. Alex and I
didn't think much of them either. But what the hell? It
was a good plug for employing us disabled people.
That's what we want, isn't it?"

"It's what we want, Art, but not the way we want it.
If anyone is seriously interested in this thing, let them
come here. We'll show them anything they want to see,

tell them anything they want to know. But we're not going to entertain people who just come to stare."

I turned back to my desk, aware that I was letting anger override reason, and not caring. "I hate flea circuses," I said, and went back to work.

During all this time we continued to expand, to take on new people and learn new skills. The assignment that pleased me most was one that offered help to other disabled people half a world away.

It began one day when I had lunch with Arthur Sulzberger of the *New York Times* and Dr. Howard Rusk, of Bellevue rehabilitation center, who was just back from Korea. Dr. Rusk was much concerned over Korean amputees—an estimated 10,000 of them among the soldiers and 20,000 more among civilians. The American Korean Foundation had asked him to survey the possibilities of sending over temporary artificial limbs so that the injured could get back to their rice paddies in time for the harvest.

"There's a terrible shortage over there of men, of materials, of almost everything," Dr. Rusk said. "If we don't help them on this, there is going to be starvation."

My interest was immediately stirred. "I'm sort of an expert," I said, "on artificial legs. I'd like to tackle that job."

"It would make a wonderful story," said Sulzberger.

"It might help to make people aware of disabled problems all over the world."

"I hoped that you'd want to try it," Dr. Rusk said. "I think it's your kind of job." He added that the specifications were tough. The legs had to be lightweight, flexible, easy to manipulate; they had to stand up under hard usage in muddy fields and over rough mountain roads. And they had to be turned out in a hurry on a very slim budget.

Dr. Rusk sent over a model constructed by one of his staff, and we went to work on it. We had the help of Brian Evans, a top flight engineer, who was loaned to us by Commander Rittenhouse at Grumman. Brian was an aluminum expert: after years of employing his knowledge to make planes fly, he used it now so that men could walk.

We made a strong peg leg from two pieces of aluminum. Screwed to it was a web-shaped foot designed to provide firm footing in wet fields. The molded stump socket at the other end of the leg was made from a fibre glass material dipped in a plastic hardener; it was hard as iron when dry, yet very light. The apparatus came in three sizes; ingenious arrangements at both top and bottom permitted further adjustments to individual size.

It was a good stout leg that would take a man where he had to go, and we produced it for 50 per cent less than the next low bidder. We got the job.

The chemical solvent we used gave off powerful

fumes, and some of the boys complained ruefully that they were getting hangovers without the benefits of getting drunk. We solved that by moving the operation out under the mulberry trees in the shop backyard. We worked on weekends, the first time in Abilities history, to meet the urgent deadline. Then, early in the operation, the contract was cancelled. The American Korean Foundation had located a Japanese firm which could do the job even quicker and cheaper.

I didn't mind losing this contract; not if someone else could beat our performance. Sometime, though, I'd like to go to Japan and see how they did it.

I'd like to go to Korea, too. I have a hunch that somewhere over there I would find Abilities limbs still being used to propel a rugged people through a rugged land. They called the limbs temporary, but we built them to last.

Sulzberger was right about the story possibilities in the rice paddy legs. The *Times* featured it, as did several other big papers, and at State Department request, "News of the Day" made a documentary film of the operation.

It added to what was now a barrage of publicity from many sources. Newspapers, magazines, TV and radio programs, trade journals in the fields of health and industry were all asking for interviews. The *Saturday*

Evening Post and *Reader's Digest* in particular, ran articles which stirred tremendous interest.

It reached the point where the shop wags referred to our makeshift little reception lobby as "the press room." More than once in the lobby I found reporters interviewing job applicants who were trying to interview me.

It was, of course, what we had set out to accomplish —a national spotlight on what could be done for disabled people. But it brought with it a heartbreaking problem for us.

I came to know with a sense of dread that every story would set the phones ringing day and night at my office and home, and bring fresh baskets of mail to be dumped on my desk. The calls and letters were of many kinds— angry, desperate or pleading, hopeful or hopeless, pathetic or gallant. But one thing they all had in common. They begged for jobs.

Some of the applicants didn't bother to write or phone. They invested their meager savings, climbed on buses or trains, and traveled hundreds of miles to present themselves at our door in the trusting faith that here at last was the answer to their prayers.

We were growing fast, so we were able to hire many. Others we put on the waiting list. But the sheer pressure of numbers forced us to turn many more away.

Patiently, over and over, we explained that Abilities could never hope to hire every disabled person who wanted to work. We were only a pilot project, a demonstration unit, to show what could be done if American business would follow our lead.

Have you ever tried to explain a pilot project to a broke, desperate, disabled man who pleads for a job?

I had to apply finally for an unlisted home phone number so that I could sleep at night.

A man from J.O.B. came in once a week to help us cope with the swelling tide of applicants. He had other duties and so he had to keep a tight schedule. Every Friday he interviewed seven people at the top of our list. It meant a long wait for the applicants but it was the best we could do.

Assisting with the job interview paper work was Ellen Vaughan of our shop. A warm-hearted, beautiful young woman, Ellen was a paraplegic as a result of childhood polio. She bore the misfortune with serene courage—in fact, she considered herself a fortunate person.

"Everything comes easy to me," she confided once. "Other people have to spend weeks or months learning to walk with braces. I put mine on and started to walk immediately. I've always been able to get along."

If Ellen wasted scant sympathy on herself, she worried much about others. It grieved her that people in need waited weeks sometimes to get an interview. And then, suddenly, the responsibility became hers. J.O.B. was very busy. They couldn't send a man one Friday. Could Ellen take over?

She could and did. She promptly called fourteen who were waiting and told them to apply at the usual time.

Having acted, she lost her nerve. It rained hard Thursday night and she prayed that the storm would continue and keep the applicants away. But they showed up, all fourteen of them. We were able to hire only four that week. Ellen had to decide.

Soon Ellen was serving as personnel director. She set up her "office" at one corner of a long, all-purpose work bench jammed up against the big double doors of the garage. It was the only space we could spare in the crowded plant.

The bench had never been intended to serve as a desk. Ellen's typewriter perched almost as high as her head. She had to reach up from her wheelchair to tap the keys. She had to contend, too, with the fact that the garage doors which served as one wall didn't quite reach the floor. Wind whistled through the gap, freezing her feet in the winter, scouring her in summer with hot, dusty blasts. Ellen never complained. She presided over her makeshift arrangement with a kind of gay dignity and marvelous ease.

The one thing she could not take in stride was saying no to people in need. Sometimes she would cry in the midst of an interview. Sometimes she would interrupt the interview and wheel across the floor on some imaginary errand while she fought to regain her composure. It became a kind of shop signal. When we saw Ellen answer a phone that wasn't ringing, we knew that she had another tough one.

Finally Ellen came to me and asked to be transferred to another assignment. She just couldn't take it any more. But after awhile she was back at her old post again as personnel director. She had discovered that the pain of saying no was more than balanced by the pleasure she found in being able to say yes.

One incident upset Ellen deeply. An attractive, well dressed woman appeared for an interview and struck a casual, lounging pose with an expensive coat draped over one arm. She appeared to have no problems at all. But as she talked, a note of rising hysteria entered her voice. She grew more and more excited. It became apparent that she was in sore need of psychiatric aid.

People persecuted her, the woman said. Her husband was trying to come between her and their child. Her last employer had fired her without reason. And then, with what she thought was a dramatic gesture, the woman threw back her coat to reveal that her left arm ended in a rounded stump. "They all hate me," she cried, "because of this!"

Ellen tried to calm her, without effect.

"I'll kill myself," the woman shouted. "I'll kill myself if I don't get this job."

Ellen stalled. She did busy things with an application blank, made soothing noises about no openings now but something might turn up later. The applicant was not deceived.

· "You're like the rest," she cried, waving the stump in Ellen's face. "You're like all the rest." As she turned to go, she flung out again the sick words, "I'll kill myself!"

The next day Ellen didn't come to work.

She spent the day at her radio, tuning the dial to every news program, checking the papers for the dreaded story that never appeared.

"Hank," she told me afterward, "we couldn't do anything for that poor woman. I know that. But still, it was I who turned her away. If she had killed herself, it was on my hands."

Another time a peddler drifted in, selling nameplate signs. They were wretched signs, ill made and over-priced, and so he traded on sympathy, which was really the only stock he had. He told Ellen his story. He was old and feeble; his children would have nothing to do with him; he was about to lose his home. Before he was finished, he and Ellen were both in tears.

She didn't buy his signs. She gave him a job.

It didn't work out. The old man was far gone in mind as well as body, in need of help that went beyond ours. We tried him everywhere, and he failed repeatedly at the simplest tasks. Two or three times I was ready to fire him, but Ellen contrived somehow to shield him each time. Finally it had to be faced. I told Ellen I would give him the bad news with the next paycheck. Then, two days before the deadline, age and illness and many troubles took their toll, and our problem employee suffered a severe attack of high blood pressure. To Ellen's vast relief and mine, he decided to quit.

While he worked at Abilities, the old man made a nameplate for Ellen as a token of gratitude. Rather than hurt his feelings, she accepted and used the unsightly thing. When he was gone I suggested that she throw it away.

Ellen gave me a rueful smile.

"If you don't mind, Hank, I think I'll keep it. It reminds me of something I need to remember."

CHAPTER NINE

THE BRIDGE OF LIES

For a year the plant had bustled with work and life.
Now, for two weeks, it would be silent and empty.
Abilities was closing down for a paid vacation.

At five o'clock on a sweltering August afternoon, I
stood at the door to watch the gang depart. They
streamed out, cheerful and exuberant, waving final fare-
wells before they went their separate ways. It was, for
many of them, the first vacation *from* something that
they had ever had.

Alex Alazraki stumped away, a cigar tilting from his
mouth at a jaunty angle. I could guess at his vacation
plans. Alex lately was showing all the signs of a man
who had met the girl.

There was no need to guess Frank Rieger's plans. His girl waited for him at the wheel of his new car; she leaned out of the window to blow him a kiss as he hurried toward her swinging on his crutches. They would spend the two weeks looking for the home they hoped to share soon.

Art Nierenberg and Jim Wadsworth left the shop together. Art had just bought a boat, and Jim was itching to try again the sailing he had known and loved in an adventurous past. They were going for a cruise on Great South Bay off Long Island.

Helen Pearson was flying to Maine to visit friends. For Helen, confined to a wheelchair, it would be the first airplane ride; it was also the first real pleasure trip she had undertaken on her own.

So they departed: many people on many errands of life. When the last one was gone, I locked the door and went home to start a crowded vacation of my own. I had a house to build.

Home, like shop, was in a converted garage. We were renting it from Dr. Yanover, the old friend and family physician who long ago had helped to stand me up on artificial legs.

The place was tucked into a corner of Doc's Long Island estate. It had been a junk-littered and all but abandoned shell of a building when Lucile and I first saw it as a young couple about to be married. Doc kiddingly suggested it as our honeymoon home and, not kidding at all, we took him up on it. Those were the housing shortage days after World War II; we were desperate for a place to live. Besides, Lucile saw in it a challenge that she could not resist. It was the kind of home a bride could remodel and rearrange to her heart's content.

With the help of a handyman, Lucile and I whipped the place into shape. I would get up at dawn, start the handyman on the day's assignment before I had to leave for my office, then return in the evening to check his progress. On weekends, Lucile and I worked together, blithely tackling all sorts of tasks we knew nothing about.

Once I cemented the bathroom plumbing into place upside down, and had to summon an expert for emergency repairs. It was in the bathroom, too, that Lucile was trapped when we hung a door from the wrong side of the jamb. The door wouldn't swing; she couldn't get out and I couldn't get in. We had a devil of a time getting the darned thing unhinged.

Building materials of all kinds were in short supply in those days. We picked up some hard-to-get fixtures from a friendly housewrecker, and obtained other items by scrounging through junk yards as far away as Connecticut. The nails we needed for walls and roof came from a ship chandler's shop in Port Washington, New

York. Those galvanized ship nails were a real find. As I whacked them into place, I knew they would last until my grandchildren were grown.

Finally, after long and loving labor, the job was done. The shell of a garage became a snug cottage just right for two. It stood on a little knoll, overlooking a view of Long Island Sound. We thought it was wonderful.

As the years passed we acquired our first three children—Nina, Donna and Lydia. The children, in turn, acquired a cat. We became involved also with an outsized Hungarian sheepdog, a shaggy, sad-eyed creature named Chico who seemed to take up an inordinate amount of space just standing around. We no longer felt snug in our little home. We felt squeezed.

Lucile's father, our beloved Poppy, was growing very frail, and we wanted to bring him and Nana to live with us. It wasn't possible in the crowded cottage. And so, reluctantly, we began to page through want ads and venture forth on half-hearted expeditions to inspect houses for sale.

Sometimes Lucile invented reasons why a particular house just wouldn't do. Sometimes I did. Finally we faced it.

"Hank," Lucile said one night, "I love this house. I don't want to move."

I felt that way, too. The place had become much more than a house. It was home.

We asked Doc to sell us the cottage, plus an acre of

ground on which to expand. He wanted a little time to think it over. He was willing enough to let the house go, but the extra acre was another matter. It would swallow up the truck garden he planted every year.

"You and your garden," I protested with a too-nervous laugh. "Every year you plant it, and every year it goes to weeds as soon as it's time to put your boat in the water. All it gets you is a lot of expensive exercise."

"Don't rush me, Hank," he said gently. "I'll think about it and let you know."

A few days later he ambled over, and stuck his head in our door. "All right," he announced drily. "I'll sell."

There was a celebration on the spot.

The $5,000 award which Baruch had maneuvered for me came in very handy now. It swelled our family bankroll just enough to finance the expansion.

On Dr. Yanover's recommendation we chose as builder a short, pot-bellied Irishman named Ed Mead. Ed was a man who defined his profession in the broadest possible terms. He was prepared to build anything, indoors or out, whether he knew anything about it or not. He had constructed a seawall for Doc on that basis and it had stood the test of time and tide.

"He's a little erratic," Doc warned us, "but one thing you can count on. If he builds it, it stays built."

Ed himself put it in a still more positive light. "Don't

yez worry about a thing," he assured us. "Ed Mead will take care of yez."

My conferences with Ed were vague, formless affairs that would have given nightmares to any other builder. Partly it was because Viscardi didn't quite know what he wanted. Partly it was Ed's own magnificent indifference to mere detail.

I needed at least five new rooms, I told him. Or maybe six. An addition might be tacked on at one end of the house to take advantage of level ground. And perhaps a balancing wing at the other end. Kind of an L to enclose the original cottage. Only not the original cottage, exactly, because the old living room had to be enlarged somehow. And while we were at it, we might want to dig into the hill for a playroom on a lower level.

Did Ed get the picture?

He nodded sagely. It was exactly his style of operation.

"Oh, yes," Lucile put in, "the whole interior will be finished in knotty pine."

That clinched the deal. All his life, Ed confided, he had wanted someone to let him finish a house in knotty pine from one end to another. This was his first opportunity. I think it would have broken his heart if we hadn't given him the job after that.

We wanted to start the job during the shop vacation. But there remained the problem of housing the Viscardis while our home was torn apart. A friend, Chuck Chiusano, offered us the use of his home during all of August while he and his family vacationed elsewhere.

Elated, I called Ed. Could he get our place in livable condition in a month's time? I got an answer that I would soon learn to recognize as a familiar refrain.

"Ed Mead will take care of yez."

On moving day I arrived home limp and late to find that Lucile was managing with her usual aplomb. Our effects were all packed and arranged in neat little rows. Grandparents and children were assembled and ready to go. Lucile piled them into the car and drove off with enough baggage to establish a rudimentary beachhead while I stayed behind to load a pick-up truck.

When Lucile returned I had the truck piled high. We jammed the rest of the stuff into the car. We were all set now—except for the dog.

Chico had been nervous all evening. Now he became frantic. He lumbered around the cottage uttering plaintive barks. He absolutely declined to go with us. Finally by main force and violence I horsed him into the back seat of the old Oldsmobile.

"Chico," I scolded, "you're a born conservative. Even before you start, you've made up your mind that wherever you're going, you're not going to like it."

Half way to the Chiusano house I remembered that I hadn't eaten. We stopped at a diner for a quick sandwich and coffee and left Chico locked in the car. He set up a fearful howling.

"What's the matter with that dog?" I asked irritably.

Lucile defended him. "He's like us, Hank. He doesn't like to leave home."

Finally, well past midnight, we arrived at our destination. I saw with relief that the house was dark. "Thank God," I said, "they're all asleep. We'll sneak in quietly and fall into the first bed we find. We can straighten things up in the morning."

But they weren't asleep. Nana met us at the door in her dressing gown. From somewhere behind her came the sound of children sobbing. Before I could manage a "What's wrong?" my usually self-possessed mother-in-law poured out her woes.

"The lights went off!" she said. "I was in the tub all soaped, and then the lights went off. Nina's crying. She says she can't go to sleep without Squeaky. And something's happened to Donna's cot. I moved it closer to the window so the child would get more air. I guess the roller fell out. Anyway, I can't find it and the bed tips every time she moves. She grabbed hold of the draperies and pulled the rod down and the curtains are dragging on the floor.

"I can't fix anything in the dark," she ended on a wail.

To Nana's laments was added a plaintive query from Poppy. "Did you bring my pillow?" Poppy couldn't sleep without his special pillow.

Lucile groped through the dark to comfort the children and take Poppy the pillow. I started striking matches to look for the fuse box. My last match had just about burned out when I found it. The lights flared up on a disordered scene.

"I'm seasick!" Donna wailed.

"No, you're not," I said firmly, and stacked two story books under the leg of her tipsy bed.

"I want Squeaky!" sobbed Nina.

"I'm sorry, Nina, but we forgot to bring your bunny."

Nina sobbed louder. Suddenly Donna wiped away her own tears and spoke severely to her elder sister. "You'll just have to go to sleep without your bunny, Nina."

"I'm glad the Chiusanos can't see what we're doing to their house," Lucile said, removing the fallen draperies.

Poppy appeared in a doorway, waving his pillow in accusing gesture.

"What's happened to my pillow? It's all wet."

Chico slunk abjectly from the room.

"Oh, Chico," Lucile said. "So that's why you howled when we were in the diner."

I wished despairingly that I was back at the office, wrestling with the simple, logical problems of running a factory. Then a fresh howl cut my reverie short.

"Daddy, daddy! I'm scared. I heard noises!"

Little bare feet came running. Donna's tear-stained little face pressed itself into my lap.

Moving out of our cottage was just a warm-up for the action that followed. The real show began when we moved back in.

Several times during that August I reminded Ed that we'd have to have some livable arrangement by the end of the month. Each time he assured me that things were proceeding nicely. I was dubious, but I didn't argue with him.

Then it was too late to argue, because the Viscardis were back in the house. Ed was there, too, taking care of us.

He had responded to my sense of urgency by starting work on six rooms at once. Naturally, none of them were finished. The dining and living rooms had been roofed but not sided. The living room had no floor. The windows weren't in. And two new bedrooms had no need of windows—they consisted at the moment of a roof and nothing more.

All the old plumbing had been ripped out and re-located, but not one fixture, essential or otherwise, had been hooked up for use.

Ed solved everything, after a fashion. He hung old tarpaulins around the place, to serve in lieu of windows in case it rained. He had his men build us a cesspool big enough for an apartment house. He dragged in with an air of triumph an old galvanized iron tub for use in bathing until he had time to finish one of the bathrooms. He shoved sawhorses and scaffolding aside to hook up our sink and stove in a rubble-strewn, unfinished kitchen. It looked like the soup kitchen in a disaster area.

Our old bedrooms were full of litter, but they did provide a place to sleep. The unfloored living room blocked the passage to these rooms, however. Ed gathered old boards and built a bridge across the gap. It was a precarious thing that dipped and swayed at every step.

"Ed Mead's Bridge of Lies," we called it.

Actually, it was wrong to label Ed's promises as lies. His trouble was an incurable optimism. He would cheerfully agree to do whatever you asked, whenever you asked it. And if he was running a bit behind schedule this week, why, next week, surely, he would be running ahead. It always came to him as a fresh surprise when next week found him even further behind.

He had promised a lot of work to a lot of people that summer, and he was constantly sending off half his crew to placate someone who was pressing him harder than Lucile and I. We became involved in a neighborhood tug-of-war with easygoing Ed as the rope.

We got mad at him, but we couldn't stay mad. Besides, the house by now was such a muddle that only Ed could straighten it out. So we learned to cope with what Lucile described as camping in.

As the weeks slid into months, the weather turned cold. We hung the tarps over open windows and across unsided rooms, piled fantastic quantities of wood in the fireplaces, and carried electric heaters about with us through the drafty rooms.

We dragged our best clothes out of trunks—there were still no closets—pressed them, and went out to parties where we forgot all about the disordered scene that awaited at home.

We grew accustomed to chill, drafty baths in the old galvanized tub. We even got used to the Bridge of Lies.

We managed. Or rather Lucile did. She took it all in easy stride as though keeping house in the midst of a construction project was the most natural thing in the world. As for Viscardi, he had long since found a measure of escape in going back to his plant.

The children loved the raucous confusion. Little Lydia would sit in her playpen, all bundled in sweaters, and pound her rattle by the hour while the men pounded nails. To this day, she prefers hammers to dolls. When the work stopped at noon, Nina and Donna would join the workmen, perching now on one knee and now on another, to chatter happily while the crew ate lunch. Occasionally, Chico would get someone's lunch first, and Lucile would replenish it from our supply.

Big Lou was a particular favorite with the children. He was a friendly, dark giant of a man with big shoulders, arms and hands; his heart was big, too. He had the genuine affection which children recognize, and he responded with infinite patience to their endless questions and demands for games. Every time he sat down, little Nina found her way to his knee.

Big Lou was a favorite of ours, too—he was an excellent carpenter. So was Burke, who was as blond as Big Lou was dark. Then there was aged Mr. Freeman. We instinctively called him Mister and never learned his first name. A tall, thin, white-haired man with fine features, he managed to look like a bank official who had momentarily donned overalls. Mr. Freeman was all business. When he had received his orders for the day, he turned off his hearing aid and worked quietly away, oblivious to everything but the wood that took beautiful shape beneath his hands.

Jasper, the painter, was not all business. He paused for a drink one morning on his way to the job and was out of commission for the next four days. Then he worked hard for a whole weekend to make up lost time. Jasper took a personal interest in making our "nutty" pine look nice. Once he discovered that one of the panels in the living room had been spliced in a way that offended his eye. He spent hours painstakingly painting in "knots" to cover the crack.

Willie, the pick-and-shovel man, was a wiry fellow, genial and obliging. A few minutes with him made it clear that he never aspired to anything more mentally taxing than his pick and shovel, but those he wielded with a right good will. Alec, a general utility man, was rough-hewn and weatherbeaten. His red face and bulbous nose were prominent features at St. Aloysius Parish Church where he ushered every Sunday.

Joe, the cement mixer, had two trademarks—I'm not sure I would recognize him without them. Rain or shine, whatever the season, Joe invariably turned up in a battered rain hat. And his pipe, burning or cold, was never out of his mouth except when he ate.

We knew them all well. We came to regard them as friends of the family who had moved in for a rather extended stay.

A season of cold, dreary rain began about the middle of November. The outer walls and windows were now in place, but the unfinished dining room floor had wide cracks giving on the playroom below, which was still open to the great outdoors. It was impossible to warm the house.

One night it stormed. The wind rose steadily, loose boards flapped and banged, and we could hear the surf pounding on Doc's seawall. We had set up a Franklin stove in the dining room. I built a roaring fire in it and we huddled around it swathed in blankets against the cold blasts that came up from the garage below.

We agreed that it would be wise for all of us to sleep in the dining room and keep the fire burning all night.

Lucile, Nina and Donna curled up on the sofa bed. I tried to bring Lydia's crib in from the bedroom, but ran into difficulties at the Bridge of Lies.

"Wait," Lucile called. "You can't roll the crib across that thing. I'll make a bed for Lydia in her play pen." She piled sofa pillows into the pen and draped blankets around it to keep out the draft.

About that time the lights went off and we had to dig out a kerosene lamp. By now the wind was really howling and I was a little concerned. I decided not to go to bed at all.

"I'll just keep my legs on and sit here with my feet up, in the big chair," I said. "That way I'll be all set to get more wood for the fire—or in case something happens."

Lucile protested that I would be dead the next day, but she finally agreed. I had to keep my legs on in order to replenish the wood, and with all that gear attached to me, I would be as comfortable in the chair as anywhere else.

My family finally fell asleep and I dozed fitfully. Several times during the night, I got up to feed the hungry stove. It was nearing morning on one of these occasions, and I happened to look out toward the Sound. There, over Doc's roof, loomed two black masts. It looked as though a big vessel was coming right up on his beach.

There was a light in Doc's bedroom. Evidently the storm had him up too, so I telephoned him.

"Hey, Doc—go look out your west window."

In a moment he was back on the phone. "Hank," he called, "get on down here. It's a big schooner."

I got into my slicker and raced down the hill. A seventy-foot schooner was indeed loose and pounding on Doc's beach. We made certain there was no life aboard, and then called the police. After that there was nothing we could do but stand around and watch that magnificent ship break up. I still have the brass capstan which I salvaged from it.

The Viscardis weathered the storm somewhat better than the schooner. Once through that, I felt that there probably wouldn't be anything worse to come, so I decided to reconcile myself to Ed Mead's pace as a builder.

By the end of November our master bedroom and its bathroom were finished at last. Every lovely, warm pine panel in place. The five of us moved into it. I hung the old galvanized tub on a nail in the cellar. We reveled in long, luxurious baths every night. We slept blissfully, sniffing the aroma of pine. And no drafts.

Then I made a mistake. It occurred to me that a grotto with Madonna and Child would add a nice touch to one corner of our garden. I said it aloud, in Ed's presence. Work on the house came to a standstill for one full week. Ed was so entranced with my idea that he put every man to work on the grotto.

"I thought you would want it for Christmas," he explained.

"I hoped we'd have the *house* by Christmas," I said pointedly.

"Now don't yez worry," he told me for the hundredth time. "Ed and the Blessed Mother will take care of yez." I guess he figured by now he could use an assist from above.

Somewhat to our surprise we did get into the living room by Christmas. The Bridge of Lies was removed, furniture was triumphantly installed in the completed room, and Lucile prepared to build a fire in the new fireplace. She was stopped short by a frightened "meow." Our cat Mehitabel had climbed into the chimney through an aperture at the base and now he couldn't find his way out again.

Lucile tried to coax him out, offering bribes of raw liver. Mehitabel refused to budge and kept up his piteous wailing. The afternoon wore on and the room grew colder. Donna wept for her cat.

At about nightfall, Lucile gave up and called on the obliging Big Lou for help. He tried to widen the hole so that he could reach in and pull the cat out. No luck. He went around to the other side and cut another hole. Mehitabel continued to squat just out of reach.

Big Lou sat down to think it over. When he returned to action it was with a heavy hammer and an air of purpose; he began to beat furiously on the metal lining of the heatolator around which the chimney is built. Kitty shot out of the fireplace like one demented. Donna took him off to the bedroom to comfort him.

We built a fine fire, the children went through the ceremony of hanging their stockings by the new fireplace, and Lucile and I relished its warmth as we installed and decorated the Christmas tree.

Lucile did not attempt to prepare Christmas dinner in the makeshift kitchen. Hospitable relatives took us in like homeless waifs for the day.

During January and early February, Ed and his men finished the rest of the rooms one by one. They hated to leave. As work neared an end, they invented things to do. One day they took time out to build a small table with stools for the children. Another time they helped me hang a ceramic of St. Francis on the big pine tree at our front door. They endlessly altered and added shelves for Lucile in the kitchen and closets.

Poppy and Nana moved into the cottage with us, and Ed's men stood by to see them comfortably settled— just in case something needed to be fixed.

Finally, when not one thing more could be found to be done, when every feature of our home was as perfect as loving skill could make it, these good men packed up their tool kits and departed. It was Lincoln's Birthday.

"You must come back in the summer," Lucile insisted. "Bring your families for a picnic in the yard."

"We will," they promised. They did, but Ed Mead

was not among them. And our beloved Poppy was not with us. Six weeks after the new house was finally finished, Poppy died during the night. Mr. Mead attended his funeral, then five days later our builder, too, was dead, of a heart attack.

He promised to take care of us, and he did. No one could ask for a better home than the one Ed Mead built for us.

CHAPTER TEN

ROOM TO GROW IN

Abilities had a housing problem, too. The once empty garage swarmed with almost a hundred workers and we were hiring new people nearly every week. Somehow we always managed to squeeze them in. But my shop foremen came to dread the hectic conferences at which the squeezing was done.

"We're taking on six new guys Monday," Viscardi would announce at a typical session. "We'll have to set up an extra bench. Now, if we can shove the harness crew back a little. . . . "

"Hey!" The anguished wail would come from the foreman of the harness section. "You've shoved my gang back three times already. If you do it again, we'll be working in the johnny."

"I guess you are pretty crowded, at that. How about the other sections? Any room in cables?"

It was the cable foreman's turn to protest: "If these new guys are midgets, Hank, they can work under our benches. I swear that's all the space we have left."

"Well, boys, we have to put them somewhere. Maybe we can steal a little space from the aisles. Let's see that floor plan again. If we reshuffle the benches and take three inches out of every aisle. . . . "

There was a limit, of course, to this kind of expansion. The aisles became so narrow and crowded that a traffic jam resulted whenever two wheelchairs met. Soon work gangs were spilling out the back door of the shop and into the yard where a faded old awning provided shelter of sorts. And the packaging department was pushed clear out of the plant. We had to rent a store building in nearby Hempstead as a temporary packaging annex.

Up to this point it was just a problem. It took a local bureaucrat to transform it into a real crisis.

A crotchety building inspector walked into our packaging annex one day, announced that we were conducting manufacturing operations in a commercial zone, and gave us two weeks to get out.

The inspector wouldn't discuss the matter with us, wouldn't listen to our pleas for a little time to find a new place. Precisely two weeks later he returned to serve a final notice of zoning violation.

I was furious—and heartsick. If the order stuck we'd

have to lay off the entire packaging crew, some two dozen people who depended on us. We couldn't possibly crowd them back into the garage.

An appeal to the zoning board was the only hope. Our attorney, Jack Coffey, thought we had solid legal grounds for contesting the decision. We decided that we would appeal to public opinion as well.

We dug into our files, pulled out case histories which showed what the packaging department meant to the people who worked there.

Alex Alazraki was assigned a role in our presentation. In a moment of inspiration, while watching the record changer on a phonograph, Alex had invented an ingenious packaging machine which Abilities now used. He would buttress our case with a public demonstration of the machine.

Nierenberg had a role, too. He would describe our entire operation, show what Abilities was contributing to the community in which we lived. I would sum up, tell what we were trying to do for the entire country.

When we were all set I tipped off some newspaper friends.

Our zoning board appearance was deliberately staged as a big production. I stalked in dramatically, arms laden with papers and briefcases. Close behind me wheeled Nierenberg, more reports and papers stacked in his lap. Behind Art stumped Alex, the packaging machine clasped in his tiny arms. And behind Alex trouped a small platoon of reporters and photographers.

The zoning board chairman took one look at the procession and drew me off to a corner.

"I think this matter can be ironed out, Mr. Viscardi. Why don't we set it aside and work out a compromise in executive session?"

Here I was, all primed for battle and the opposition was retreating without a shot. On a sudden impulse I decided that I'd fire my guns anyway, just for effect.

"If you don't mind, Mr. Chairman, we have a case to make. We'd like to state it for the public record."

For two hours at least we stated our case. Several times board members broke in, trying to speed the hearing to an early close. We kept right on talking. Once or twice Attorney Coffey tugged at my coattails, signaling that enough was enough. I shook him off. Doggedly we ploughed through the statistics, the case histories, the demonstration, the appeals to reason and common sense. Finally I snapped shut the last briefcase. The defense rested.

Our newspaper friends jumped on it, which was part of what I had in mind. The press the next day splashed stories which did Abilities no harm at all.

More important, we won the concession we had to have. The board granted us a six months extension on the order to vacate.

The zoning board ruling was a reprieve, not a solution. We still had to contend with our ever-growing need for space. Abilities board meetings and planning sessions revolved ever more urgently around our need for a larger plant.

I was eager to make the move. The old garage had served its purpose; now we were ready for better things. I had visions of a new building, handsome and spacious, which would serve as a bright symbol of disabled achievement. I wanted a place big enough to house both the shop and the medical research we hoped to sponsor at some future date.

Nierenberg had some ideas on the subject, too. He wanted a building equipped with swimming pool, gym and recreation room for off-hours use. Those facilities would serve more than morale purpose since many of our employees had a medical need to exercise neglected muscles. High also on Art's list was a modern plant cafeteria to provide full course hot meals at noon.

Success was intoxicating; anything seemed possible now. So we planned big, and dreamed boldly, and designed on paper a beautiful plant. Then I went shopping for land and buildings and the bright bubble collapsed. What we wanted cost too much.

Industrial property was at a premium on booming Long Island. Poor locations were being offered at $30,000 an acre, the good locations were fantastically high. For months I chased up and down the Island, checking possible sites, and after every trip I mentally dismantled another feature of our future plant. Before long I was looking for just a place to go on working.

I got a tip once that a former airfield hangar was being offered for rent. It was big enough, and the price was right. The location, however, suggested problems. The surrounding area was being developed into a huge industrial park and shopping center. We might be overwhelmed in the crush of traffic. I arranged for a test crew to spend a few days there and try it out.

"How was it?" I asked when the crew reported back.

"Like working in Grand Central Station," the foreman said. "Only worse. You can't fight your way in or out of the place when the rush is on."

Reluctantly, I crossed off that possibility and resumed the search.

About this time we received two very generous, wholly unexpected offers of help. A business group wanted to give us a big tract of land on Long Island. And the Bricklayers Union on Long Island was willing to put up a new building without charge if we furnished the materials.

It was tempting, enormously tempting. We could at one stroke end our struggles and achieve our most optimistic goals. But I held back. I was afraid that we might get involved with other organizations, become subject to policies and programs that were not our own. We had fought too hard for identity to risk losing it now.

Some of our directors thought my fears were foolish. There was hot debate at a board meeting.

"Why not be sensible?" one director urged. "It's not even a question of compromise. These are public spirited offers with no strings attached."

"The strings," I replied, "would be in our minds. If we accept these gifts we'll always feel that we owe something to our benefactors. Our only obligation should be to ourselves."

"Hank," another director grumbled, "you're too damned independent for your own good. What are you trying to prove?"

"I'm trying to prove that we *are* independent," I shot back. "If we start leaning on other people, it might get to be a habit."

In the end we rejected both offers with thanks, and continued to look for a place that would be entirely ours. And then a solution emerged in our own back yard. Milton Beddell, our landlord, offered to sell us the garage plus an empty lot next door. It would provide space enough for a plant addition.

Beddell's price was $75,000. We thought he was too high. We dickered awhile. Finally it was agreed that he would build the addition in return for a suitable increase in rent. We signed a new lease.

It wasn't anything like the shop we had dreamed of, but it would do for the moment. And there was still plenty of time to make the dreams come true. Abilities was only two years old.

We closed the shop for our second paid vacation at the end of July. As our people departed, a construction gang moved in to put up a concrete block addition.

Viscardi hovered around, nervous from past experience with building crews and their schedules, but this time there was no need to worry. The work went so swiftly that from one day to the next you could see the shop grow.

New wiring was installed free by members of the International Brotherhood of Electrical Workers. "The bosses had the fun last time," they said, "now it's our turn." That gesture of friendship we were glad to accept.

In two weeks we returned to a shop four times as big as the one we had left. And what a difference it made! Materials were stacked neatly in convenient places, not piled helter-skelter underfoot. People no longer huddled shoulder to shoulder over cramped and cluttered benches. We could get through the aisles. We reveled in the luxury of space.

The size of the shop proved a problem to some who walked with crutches and braces, but that was easily overcome. We furnished wheelchairs for everyone who had ambulatory disabilities.

Polio-crippled Ronnie LeMieux lacked the hand strength to propel his wheelchair across the floor. The ever ingenious Jim Wadsworth rigged up a small battery-powered motor so that Ronnie could go whizzing along at the touch of a button. For Alex Alazraki, Wadsworth built a motorized cart with tiller controls.

There was room in the place for a few comforts and conveniences. We built a big snack bar and installed it in the middle of the shop floor; a gaily striped awning added a carnival touch. And we made a small beginning on the recreation program. A paved area behind the shop provided for ping-pong, shuffleboard and a bowling game which could be played from wheelchairs.

A fine, big room was set aside for medical care. Looking at it I realized how far we had come since the days when Doc Glasser made his examinations at the bench or, sometimes, in the men's room which he called his "private suite."

A full-time nurse was in charge of the medical room; she was trained to give corrective exercises under a doctor's direction. A portable iron lung stood by for emergency use at the plant or in a worker's home. That was a memorial to Roslyn Caputo, an Abilities employee who died at her home one night when a bad cold proved too much for her polio-weakened lungs.

Another special feature was a dental clinic, complete with $8,500 worth of new equipment. Many of our people had serious dental problems as part of general poor health; some of them found it impossible to visit a dentist's office if the trip involved climbing even a few steps. We arranged for a local dentist, Dr. Jerry Bloom, to come in and use our facilities one evening a week.

The clinic brought pained outcries from members of the local dental society. They summoned Dr. Bloom and accused him of "unethical practice." He couldn't see anything unethical about it and despite heavy pressure he stood his ground. Then he found himself with no ground to stand on. A state inspector informed him that he would lose his license if he did not "cease and desist."

"Well, boy, they've got you," I said when he gave me the news. "You have to eat. But let's get together with these people and see if we can't talk sense."

I asked a dental committee to visit the shop and they proved unexpectedly conciliatory. Perhaps on second thought they were a little ashamed of what had been done. Or maybe someone simply hadn't given the matter any first thought to begin with. In any case we worked out a compromise. We would draw on a panel of local dentists, including Dr. Bloom, and each patient would select the panel member he wanted. A fee schedule was worked out. The dentists withdrew their opposition and our setup was duly approved by the state inspector.

Meantime the dental chair was not going to waste. A barber used it after plant hours to cut the employees' hair. He did a brisk business.

There was no trouble about that. The barbers didn't have a society.

Our new nurse was Marguerite Parenti, a mature, motherly woman who had a faculty for keeping her arms around our people. They loved her. And almost at once we had need of her services.

One morning she stuck her head in my office door. "Mr. V., are you good at problems?"

She was worried about an epileptic we had just hired. The man had assured us that his seizures were under control.

"I'm afraid he lied," Marguerite said. "I have been talking to him and I feel that he's under great pressure from tensions at home. I don't think he's taking his control drugs. What's worse, I suspect that he suffers from frequent *gran mal* seizures."

That could be trouble. He was a husky young man; in violent seizure he might be dangerous to others. Still, we had been getting excellent results from other epileptics. Maybe Marguerite's fears were exaggerated.

"Often," I said, "we worry about things that never happen. Let's give him a few days to settle down and see how things work out."

But that afternoon it happened. Art summoned me, urgency in his voice.

"That new epileptic is in a hell of a seizure, Hank. You had better come quick."

I found the new man on the floor, a small knot of people gathered around him. Marguerite was on her knees giving quiet orders. She had assigned volunteer assistants so that two men held each leg, one man each arm. She held the patient's head.

Beside Marguerite to offer aid and advice was Abilities foreman, Sal Fortunato. Sal knew about seizures from having them.

"Now," Sal said. "See the finger twitch. Get ready." The patient convulsed as though an electric shock had coursed through his body. He hurled up from the floor, was pressed down again by many hands.

It went on like that for two hours. The people who were needed stood by to help. The others went quietly on with their work.

We moved the man to the medical room where the struggle continued. Finally he was still. Then he was conscious. Marguerite tucked a blanket around his shoulders.

"What will you do with me?" he asked. "I guess I lose my job."

"No," I said. "It's not like that. If you can prove to me that under medical care your seizures can be controlled, you can come back. I promise. Now don't worry about your job. We have sent for an ambulance. We're going to send you home to get well."

"Please," he begged. "Don't send me home. Let me stay here."

"The ambulance is waiting. You have my promise. Believe in me and I will try to help you."

He was gone.

"What of the family?" I asked Marguerite.

"A brother was with the ambulance," she said. "The mother will contact you."

The mother was there waiting early the next morning when I arrived at the office. A tired, bitter looking little woman, she was obviously seeking to bolster her morale with over-dress and too much makeup. Her hair was splotched with several shades of dye.

"You have killed my boy!" she said shrilly. "I hope you realize what you have done."

"I don't understand. He had some violent seizures here yesterday but he was all right when he left. We sent him home in an ambulance."

"Yes," she said bitterly. "They brought him to me. Then left me alone. He had another fit. I went for help. When I came back he had turned on the gas and was unconscious on the kitchen floor. The police came and took him away."

"You mean he's dead. I can't tell you how sorry. . . . "

"He's not dead," she interrupted angrily. "But because of the suicide attempt I'm having him committed to a mental institution. He's as good as dead."

Before I could speak again she had rushed out, sobbing and cursing.

Dr. Glasser checked into it, made sure that the young man was assigned to a hospital where he would have the best possible treatment. We learned in the process that the youth's family had tried several times to shunt him off to a mental institution. The shop episode, plus the attempted suicide, had presented the excuse they apparently needed for committing him again.

I had a long talk with Marguerite about the situation.

"You know about the family?" I asked.

"I know a lot. The rest I can guess. It's a shame, too, a real shame. With a little luck and a lot of love and understanding the kid might have made it. The way it was, he didn't have a chance."

"It's my fault," I said angrily. "I should never have sent him home. I should have sent him straight to a hospital."

She laid a gentle hand on my shoulder. "Don't blame yourself. I'm sure it was too late to make any difference. The hospitals will get him now and maybe they can do something for him. We can't help them all."

"No," I conceded, "we can't. But it's worth trying for, isn't it?"

She smiled warmly. "It is. Excuse me now, boss, I have some temperatures to take."

A few weeks later family trouble brought more grief. It began with a telephone ringing shrilly one night to wake me from an exhausted sleep.

A local businessman was calling. His voice was strained, angry sounding.

"I am sorry to trouble you at this late hour but I am

deeply worried about a matter that is terribly important to me."

"What can I do to help?"

"Nothing, probably, but I think you should know that my daughter has eloped with one of your paraplegics."

I smothered the retort that rose to my lips. It wasn't *my* paraplegic, only a man who worked at my shop. A man who had as much right as any other to his private life. Still, the girl's father had a right to be concerned.

"Who is the man?" I asked.

"I don't know," he said. "That's why I'm calling you."

"I'll find out," I said, "and call you back."

I phoned Art. He didn't know who it was, but he had a hunch that it might be Bill Graham. Bill had been dating a young college girl lately.

Bill didn't have a phone. Wearily I dressed, strapped on my legs, and went to his house. As soon as I arrived I knew the hunch was right. It was 2 A.M., but the lights were all on.

Bill's anguished mother met me in the doorway.

"He's gone," she cried. "He ran off with that girl, and you are responsible. Why couldn't you leave him alone? When he came back from the war he had his pension and me to take care of him. Then you came along and made him think that he can live like other people. How can he? Can he be a husband to that girl? Can she take care of him as I did?"

"If they love each other, they can try," I said.

"It won't work," she answered tearfully. "It can never work. Oh, my poor boy. You have filled his head with impossible dreams. You have created a monster and some day you will answer for it." She slammed the door in my face.

It was almost daybreak when I got home again and phoned the girl's father to pass on the news. He answered on the first ring. He must have been waiting tensely by the phone.

"She's so young," he protested. "She doesn't know the problems she's taking on. We didn't even have a chance to meet the boy."

"I'm sorry. I wish there was something I could do to help."

"Perhaps," he said stiffly, "if you think about it you will consider that you have already done enough. Good night." He hung up.

I thought Lucile was sleeping but she stirred as I slid into bed, then reached out to enfold me in her arms.

"Have I created a monster, Lucile? Did I wreck the lives of those kids?"

"Darling," she whispered, "don't let me hear you say monster again. Did I marry a cripple or did I marry the man I love? To our little girls, are you an amputee or their daddy, the greatest man in the world? Close your eyes now and sleep. Tomorrow there is work to do, God's work, and I must help you do it."

It was a relief to get back to mundane plant problems. Like urinals, for instance. A labor inspector came around and charged us with having insufficient urinals for the number of people employed. We countered with the fact that a large number of the workers were using not the regular facilities but individual prosthetic urinals which we supplied. We convinced him, finally, but it took a lot of talking. The labor department man didn't think it was a urinal unless it flushed.

We had a time with the defense department security man, too. He wanted to fingerprint everyone in the plant before giving us clearance for a certain defense job.

There was a momentary contretemps over an Abilities employee who had no hands. The security agent said that could be worked out easily enough. He'd settle for toe prints.

Then he came to Alex Alazraki.

"No fingers," Alex announced. "No toes, either." Alex paused, appearing to be considering the problem gravely, then went on with an air of deadpan innocence. "It happens, however, that I do have one complete appendage. I'd be glad to give you a print of that."

The security man was wholly undone. Dispensing

with prints of any description he agreed to clear us for the job.

Our second anniversary party was a turkey dinner served community style at the local high school auditorium. Once again we took stock of achievements:

Our wages were up. Employee earnings for the year amounted to $198,000, all of it new wealth poured into the community by men and women who had existed before on public relief or private charity.

We had produced $400,000 worth of goods. That was double the first year's effort.

Best of all, we had on hand 121 new contracts from a dozen big firms. Our future looked very bright.

Dr. Howard Rusk quite unexpectedly arrived and paid us a birthday tribute. "You have exploded," he said, "a spiritual force that is greater than atomic energy. We, the so-called normal people, can never compete with you, because we have never been put to the test. We will never know what it is like to run so fast, so far, so hard."

The birthday party closed with a triumphant ceremony in which Alex Alazraki was wheeled up to the head table to stand beside me. Alex, as I had before him, had long stumped through life at belt-buckle level, only three feet tall. Now, with help from Abilities, he had just completed the slow, painful, expensive process of being fitted for artificial limbs.

He was in a wheelchair because he did not yet trust his unfamiliar limbs to carry him through the big auditorium. But when he reached the head table he planted both feet firmly on the floor. He braced himself for a moment, gave a quick, hard push to shove the wheelchair away, and stood up, man sized. A great roar of applause rose up from the audience as Abilities saluted one of its own.

If there was a dry eye in the house, I couldn't spot it through my own mist-shrouded eyes.

When the cheers died away, Alex led us in reciting the Abilities Credo. "I seek opportunity, not security. . . . I will not trade my dignity for a handout. . . . It is my heritage to think and act for myself. . . . "

Alex took long steps on his new legs before another year passed. He married a fine young woman. It was my proud honor to be best man at their wedding. In due course, Alex was dispensing cigars and wisecracks as he announced the birth of a daughter. And this time nature was kind. Little Rica Lillian Alazraki was a beautiful baby, perfectly formed.

I wish the story of Alex could end on that note—but it cannot, quite. For shortly afterwards, a severe pressure area developed on one of his stumps. It made continued use of the new limbs inadvisable. He could wear them only occasionally.

It was a hard blow for him. Only those who have shared his misfortune can know how much he wanted those legs. But he took the bad news without a whimper.

"Sue loves me for what I am," he said when it happened, "and the baby will do the same." He laughed. "I'll put the legs on at special times, like when I want to impress the relatives."

Alex's legs were one of our most successful failures.

As Abilities grew and prospered, we became more formal and disciplined; much of the old family atmosphere was lost. It was part of the price we paid for success. A few of our workers found it hard to adjust; some were not able to make the change.

Among those who dropped out was a woman named Ida. Middle-aged and suffering from back injury, she was one of those people who have to be coaxed and babied along. Even the spur of a child to support could not rouse her from the endless contemplation of her troubles and ills.

When a small package fell and struck her a glancing blow, Ida insisted that she was painfully injured. Exhaustive medical examination revealed nothing wrong but for days she limped around the place, looking hurt. And she protested constantly that shop boss Nierenberg was too harsh and demanding. After one argument with Art, she came to me with her laments.

"Ida," I said, "Art's in charge of production. If you can't work for him, you can't work for me. You can quit or stay, it's up to you, but we're not going to have a UN debate around here every time someone asks you to get on with a job." Whereupon, she quit in a huff.

A dozen others quit or were fired. That, of course, only proved we were "normal"; it happens in every shop. The failures were surprisingly few, however, and they were more than balanced by those who made good.

Some left the shop not in defeat but in triumph, going on to better jobs or new careers. We encouraged that, though it played hob with well organized work crews. We "graduated" three or four almost every month.

Anna Esposito was one of those who used Abilities as a springboard to a new life. Anna was 42 when she came to us, painfully crippled by rheumatoid arthritis, and totally untrained for work of any kind. She was also alone in life; her marriage had broken up during her long affliction. She was determined to be self-supporting though her hands were so stricken that she could not flick a light switch.

We took care of Anna's hand problem by rigging up a few bench devices. Anna did the rest with her own indomitable spirit. She achieved a quiet success, became a dependable worker who earned steady raises. Faithfully she paid back bills that had piled up during the eight years she spent on Relief.

Most people who had experienced Anna's beating in life would have clung desperately to the security she had now achieved. Anna, however, had very little in common with most people. After three years she became restive with assembly line tasks. Her excellent record at Abilities helped her to get a proofreading job which appealed to her more. There was a small party for her when she left. A little later her friends rejoiced to learn that Anna had made still another fresh start. She married a man who had also left our shop to achieve success in another field.

There were others who stayed on at Abilities and grew with the company, developing new skills to meet our expanding needs. Lou Blersch was one of those. In just two years he rose from a disabled ex-filling station mechanic to become a top executive in what by then was a million dollar operation. Along the way he discovered some important things about himself.

Lou was a blond giant of a guy, rugged and masculine. During army service he joined the paratroops, then lost both legs, above the knees, in a training camp accident. It gave a bitter twist to his independent spirit. He became for a time like a wounded wild thing that snarls defiance and strikes out at those who seek to help.

He asked his young wife to divorce him—for her own good, he told her—but she had spunk and refused to leave him.

When he was released from the hospital he returned to the filling station job he had held before. It was tough going. Moreover, he insisted on taking a cut in pay. He thought he was worth less now and he had a horror of trading on sympathy.

Lou's self-imposed pay limitation did not work out. He was forced to borrow from his boss almost every week; often at week's end he was so deep in debt that he had to hand back the entire paycheck. Then the boss would fill Lou's car with free gas to help him out. That made him mad, so he quit.

He was turned down repeatedly when he tried to find another job. Once he had a job won when the man who was hiring said, "I'll show you the shop." They walked across a room, opened a door, and there were five steps, going up.

Lou's skill with artificial legs wasn't quite up to climbing steps, so he returned to his car for his crutches. When he came back, the employer said, "I'm sorry, but we can't take a man in your condition. There's too much risk."

Too much risk! The cautious employer was safeguarding from a five-step hazard a man who had jumped out of airplanes without batting an eye. It was a fine irony which Lou at the moment was in no position to appreciate.

After several such experiences, Lou holed up in his apartment in brooding despair. His wife was frantic. Then they read of Abilities and with her encouragement he tried again.

We hired him, and he worked out fine. He picked up the routine in a couple of days; within two weeks he had earned two raises. He relaxed and unwound, became one of the boys. But close beneath the surface a hot anger still boiled. In shop give-and-take one day, another employee called him a dirty name. When I looked up through the window in my office, Lou had lifted his one-legged opponent clear off the floor with one huge paw and was cocking the other fist to demolish him.

I broke it up. "Young man," I told him, "if that ever happens again, you're through."

He turned white, then red, clenching his fists. He wanted to belt me, but he also wanted to keep his job. The second desire was a little stronger. He went back to his bench.

Lou settled down after that to become one of the best men we ever hired. He was, among other things, a mechanical wizard and a bear for work. He ran himself so hard that we had to order him into a wheelchair. The artificial limbs could never move him about as freely and as fast as he now needed to go.

In about three weeks we put him in charge of his bench. He protested that; he had become firm friends with Eddie who bossed the bench before him and he didn't want to be promoted over Eddie's head. But we needed crack leadmen and we didn't give him a choice. Pretty soon he was a section boss, overseeing twenty men. Then foreman, running crews of fifty to a hundred. He became a trouble shooter on jobs no one else could do anything with.

Lou had a hard time recognizing himself as a man who had grown out of overalls. He came to work sometimes dressed as though his principal duty was still to climb under cars and drain out the grease. He maintained for many months a massive indifference to the dull necessities of paper work.

Once while resisting a promotion he waved his big, dirty hands in my face. "I can do things with these," he said. "I'm a hands man. But I'm not a head man. Don't push me out of my class."

"Your class," I told him, "is job man. You get things done. As long as you do that, I don't give a damn how."

He continued to insist that he was not a front office type, and he continued to advance through his ingrained desire to lick anything that stood in his way. Finally he squeezed into a white collar, and found that it fit. He became plant manager, responsible to Vice President Nierenberg for a production crew of more than three hundred people.

After years of anguish over a ruined body, Lou Blersch discovered that he had a first class mind.

A lot of changes were going on. One of them began the day Art Nierenberg poked his head into my office to announce that a shop committee wanted to see me. Close behind him trouped half a dozen of our key people.

I swivelled around. "What is it, boys? Not a strike delegation, I hope."

Art grinned. "Don't give us ideas. What we came to discuss is a credit union."

The employees had calculated that a shop credit union could build up funds at a rate of something like $500 a week. It would help them to save money, give them something to borrow against in times of emergency. It could also provide a banking service for those who had difficulty in getting to a commercial bank by crutch or wheelchair. I thought it was a fine idea.

"It's your baby," I said. "Go ahead and set it up. The company will make a deposit to get things started."

The employees contacted the agency which regulates credit unions. A government representative, a Mr. Prescott, paid us a call. He was a precise little man, neat and fussy, who looked as though he had long since reduced all questions of life to a bookkeeper's equations. I could see at a glance that our setup gave pause to his orthodox mind.

Prescott met with the shop committee in the lobby just off my office. Things went smoothly enough until he remarked that, of course, the credit union's loans could not be insured.

That was a serious blow. If anything gives a borrower peace of mind, it's the knowledge that insurance will lift the debt burden from his family in case he dies or becomes unable to work.

"How come no insurance?" Art asked.

Prescott made a discreet, throat clearing sound. "Well, after all, you are not insurable. With the exception of Mr. Viscardi, everyone here is already disabled."

"Oh boy!" Wadsworth whooped. "You haven't seen the boss with his pants off, have you?"

I overheard the exchange and came charging out of my office to back the boys up. I decided on shock tactics.

"Mr. Prescott," I said, "I'd like to hear you sing in high C."

He looked puzzled. "I can't sing at all. I don't know what you're talking about."

"I'm talking about disability," I told him. "You say you can't sing. That makes you totally and permanently disabled for an opera career. You're probably not fit to pitch for the Yankees, either. But you are able to work at your trade. Well, so are we. We're entitled to operate under the same rules that apply to everybody else."

The argument shook him. He had supposed that this disability question was all neatly settled, like the principles of bookkeeping, with one set of people on the credit side and another set of people marked off to debit. Now it was all mixed up. He started to answer several times, but couldn't seem to find the words. Finally, in a kind of shock, he agreed that our loans were good enough to rate insurance. Ultimately we received a favorable ruling from his superiors.

The credit union made a big difference in many lives. You could riffle through the account books, noting money borrowed and saved, and find a human drama in almost every item.

There was, for instance, the $200 loan to Rose Carey.

Rose was a plump, blue-eyed blonde, a victim of polio. She was totally paralyzed in her right arm, partially paralyzed in the left, unable to bend at the waist. Surgeons had "fused" her spine, linking the bones together with a steel bar, as a desperate remedy for a weakened back.

She was stricken at age 12, and dropped out of school at 16. For the next nineteen years she seldom stirred from her home. She puttered about in her wheelchair, read a lot, sewed, helped her mother with occasional chores. She lay abed until noon usually. There was not much point in starting the day any earlier than that.

At 35 she came to Abilities. Her schedule now became very different. She got up at 5 A.M. in order to allow time for the laborious process of dressing herself and then the long journey to the plant. She put in her eight hours as a solderer, spent at least another hour getting home again. It added up to about thirteen hours a day. She loved it.

Rose's brother drove her to work every morning and picked her up every night. That was a considerable inconvenience to him; it also was a chafing limitation to her newly won independence. And so at the first opportunity Rose borrowed $200 as down payment on a car with special controls. Within a week she had learned to drive.

Rose's freedom of movement is still very limited. Someone has to lift her and her wheelchair in and out of the car at each end of the trip. But in between those two points she is as mobile as anyone on the road.

You have to be immobile for most of your life to know what that's worth.

Chet Krakowski's request for a loan was a masterpiece of terse statement. On his application blank, under Reasons For Loan, he scrawled "Need the money."

He needed it urgently. A disastrous accident had flattened him both physically and financially.

A construction worker, the father of two young children, Chet was doing fine in life until one night a hot-rod driver roared around a corner and ground him under careening wheels. The driver didn't stop to see what he had done. Chet was left on the pavement with two badly crushed legs.

He was in the hospital for two and a half years. He received some insurance compensation but not nearly enough to take up the slack. His wife scraped and saved, even cutting down discarded clothes of the nine-year-old boy to fit the four-year-old girl, but every month the Krakowskis fell a little farther behind on their bills.

Their only good fortune was that Chet didn't lose a single unnecessary day in getting back into action. He read about Abilities and filed a job application while he was still under treatment. His medical release coincided with one of our many expansions. On a Friday evening he rolled away from the hospital in a wheelchair and the next Monday morning he rolled into our shop to start learning a new trade.

He still had big problems, of course. The long siege had exhausted both his cash and his credit. He would repair his fortunes in time but his children couldn't stop growing until he caught up. The patched up, hand-me-down garments could not suffice for another reason. The credit union advanced the $100 he had to have for new clothes.

Nancy Evans signed up for what can only be described as a luxury loan. A real splurge. She felt that she had one coming.

Nancy was a typist, and a good one, though five of her fingers were vestigial stumps. You would not have judged her handicapped if you had listened to her work; the tattoo she beat on the machine compared favorably with that of a ten-finger expert. But before she came to us she could never get an office job. Her husband had a handicap, too. A former bookkeeper, he was reduced to neighborhood caretaker tasks because he was "over-age." His income barely met their rent. So Nancy worked days, and he worked nights, and between them they struggled as best they could to bring up a 13-year-old son. There wasn't much room in their regime for pleasant living.

To Nancy a kind of stigma attached to the family's misfortunes; "humiliating" was a word which crept often into her speech. She was fiercely determined that for the boy at least it would some day be better. When the credit union opened for business, she borrowed $350 and sent the youngster to a swank summer camp.

She got her money's worth. I don't know how well the boy liked the camp, but Nancy loved it. For weeks she read and reread the latest camp communique at every Koffee Klatch and lunch hour session. Then she would return to her desk, attacking her work with flourish and vigor, content in the knowledge that for once a member of the Evans family was "having things nice."

Len Lobue took out a whole series of loans. If you knew a little of his background you could almost trace his progress through life by the way he borrowed, paid back, and borrowed again.

He was 19 when he came to us, a skinny, tow-headed little wisp of a guy who walked with the rolling gait of a drunken sailor. It was a near miracle that he was able to walk at all. Len was born without hip sockets. Until he was six years old his mother trundled him around in a baby carriage. Rolling along in that ill-chosen contrivance, peering timidly out at the careless children who hooted at him when he passed, and at the careless adults who gawked, Len developed a defensive shyness that never left him. His speech to this day reverts to a hesitant mumble in moments of stress.

Doctors tried to correct his defect but the first operation was not successful. Worse, someone at the hospital mistook his shyness and lack of development for abnormality of another kind. For months he was a neglected waif in a poorly tended mental ward.

A second operation went better. A socket was built into one hip and Len learned to shamble along on crutches, dragging one stiff leg behind him. Much later the second socket was constructed and he was able to throw the crutches away.

Len was sixteen by this time. His parents had separated and he was left without strong family ties. He drifted out of high school after his freshman year, lived in a succession of shabby rooms while he ran through a series of low paid jobs. He worked as a porter, starched shirts in a laundry, ran an elevator, was a florist's assistant in charge of counting and grading the flowers. We started him as a cafeteria messboy but within six months he had advanced to an electronics bench.

Len's first loan went for a TV set. He lived alone, and it filled a big void in his life.

Pretty soon he was sharing an apartment with two other young men who worked at Abilities. A new loan helped to furnish the place. Then the others moved out to start families and Len set up his own establishment.

Once he borrowed to buy new clothes. That, for Len, was quite a development. When he joined Abilities his sartorial style was only a cut above that of the Bowery.

Finally he took a good-sized loan to buy a big, shiny new refrigerator. That raised intriguing questions. Len sustained his slight body on very little food.

"How come the big refrigerator?" I asked him one day. "You eating more these days?"

"Nope," he replied in that abashed mumble of his. "There's going to be more people eating at my place." Len was getting married to one of the girls in the plant.

What with marriages and babies, it was getting to be quite a productive shop.

Laura Altobelli never asked for a loan. She used the credit union to build up her savings. There was a story behind that, too.

Laura was an intense young woman, enormously plucky behind a diffident exterior, and tragically disabled even by Abilities standards. She had survived a cruel succession of the worst blows life can deal out.

The first tragedy was polio at age two. It left her with two paralyzed legs, one paralyzed arm, a humped and contorted spine.

It was a big immigrant family, the mother died young, and the children had to look after each other while the father worked. That led to the second disaster. One day crippled little Laura, crawling about, fell into a tub of boiling water. She emerged from that experience of pain and terror with one blind eye, a face scarred almost beyond recognition, and a crippled elbow on the arm which polio had spared.

Laura attended school for awhile in a wicker wheelchair but after five years that contact with the outside world ceased. Her father died. She went to live with a married sister. Laura crawled about the floor of her sister's home, dragging her paralyzed legs, scrubbing and polishing and caring for babies, pulling herself up on tubs to wash out the diapers. She wore herself out trying to be useful, trying to justify her miserable existence to herself.

When she was 25, someone got her to a hospital. She was operated on, preparatory to being fitted with leg braces. The hospital neglected to send a notice when it was time for the second step in the medical procedure and no one followed up to see why. After awhile it was too late. Laura's legs shrivelled beyond hope of repair.

Finally fate did Laura a favor. Her brother married a warm-hearted, generous woman who offered Laura a new home and made her feel welcome and loved. She responded with something close to adoration. No one was more thrilled than Laura when the couple announced that they were expecting their first baby. And no one was more devastated than she when the little boy was born blind. All the ache and anguish in her heart went out to the helpless infant.

A doctor suggested agencies which could help the boy, and the family inquired if there were not agencies for Laura, too. By that torturous circumstance she discovered the State Division of Vocational Rehabilitation and was referred at last to our shop.

You had to guess that this maimed, frightened woman had in her any strength of spirit. She could not express it. Not in words. She shrank back in her wheelchair, recoiling from questions, seeming ready to flee at any moment. But she expressed a lot with her hands. When we tried her on packaging she went at it with astonishing zeal. The first day she packaged more than 300 units; within weeks she had pushed it up to 1,000 a day.

Employment did things for Laura. Her shattered face took on new life. She made friends. At her sister-in-law's suggestion she invited a young couple from the plant to dinner at her home. It was the first time in her life that Laura had ever given a party.

She spent her paychecks with reckless abandon at first, lavishing presents on her brother's family, on her new friends, on casual acquaintances at the slightest provocation. The gift-giving was carried to embarrassing lengths. It was as though she were saying that presents were the only thing of value she had to offer.

There was an emotional crisis when Laura was transferred from packaging to learn electronics. Away from
her familiar first job she was overwhelmed by insecurity.
A thoughtless remark from a co-worker hurt her deeply.
She brooded, wept, ruined parts, became a problem to
her foreman. Finally she took sick and stayed home.
On her sick bed, she wrestled it out. When she returned
she was prepared to do whatever had to be done in
order to hang on to her hard won new life.

She changed in other ways, too. She was still eager
for friendship, but she no longer sought it by deluging
others with needless gifts. She discovered herself as a
person worth investing in.

Every cent she could spare now went into two funds.

One fund was for Laura. She was planning to buy a
new car.

The other fund was for the blind nephew. The time
will come when he will need money for special training
and Laura means to be sure that nothing is lacking.

Meantime Laura gives the boy something no fund can
provide. She is teaching him how to live with adversity.

I have seen how she helps him cross an unfamiliar
room. Poised at one end of the room, arms outstretched,
she calls to him as the four-year-old gropes and hesitates
and gropes again until he finds the way.

"You can do it," Laura calls to him, her voice offering
strength and assurance and guidance and love. "You can
do it."

CHAPTER ELEVEN

REACHING OUT.

By the end of our third year, I was itching to expand again. Something bigger this time than a new shop. I had dreams of a new program.

I wanted to convert Abilities into a national center for the study of disabled problems. A center for medical research on what the ill and injured are able to do. A center for industrial research on the cash value of disabled skills. A teaching and training institute which would pass on to others what we had learned about the work cure method of salvaging lives.

A program, in short, to help the millions of disabled people who weren't fortunate enough to hold Abilities jobs.

We couldn't finance the effort on the scale required, but we could provide the human laboratory. Perhaps the funds could be obtained elsewhere, from private contributions. For this goal I was willing to bury even my stout prejudice against asking for money.

Full of enthusiasm, I called a special board meeting to expound the idea. The reception was unexpectedly cool.

"This calls for donations," one director said. "I thought you were against that, Hank."

"I'm against donations for Abilities," I replied. "We're a business; we have to operate competitively to prove that disabled workers can earn their keep in a business world. But the research center would be a separate entity. There's no reason why it shouldn't be endowed like any other public service foundation."

"How much would this thing cost?" someone wanted to know.

I shrugged. "There's no limit. We'd be tackling one of the biggest jobs in America today. If we could raise half a million dollars, a hundred thousand even, we could accomplish wonderful things.

"We'll need a new building soon," I added, quite casually and without having thought it through. "Let's plan it to house a real research and teaching program. Considering what is at stake we can't afford not to raise the necessary money."

Heads wagged at this cavalier dismissal of mere money. These were conservative business men, men who believed in us and in what we were doing, but hard-headed business men, nevertheless.

One board member objected that we were taking on much more than we could hope to handle. Another chimed in to say that we were doing the essential thing now, providing jobs and setting an example for others. Why not stick to our last?

Board Chairman Bassett listened quietly as usual without saying much. Now he leaned back in his chair with an air of decision.

"Hank," he said gently, "this goes pretty far afield. Aren't you trying to do the government's job?"

"I claim that it's everybody's job, especially ours," I said. "Anyway, no one else is doing it. I think we know more than anyone about practical, down to earth work for the disabled. All I'm asking is that we let the rest of the world in on our secret."

They weren't convinced. The faces around the table wore the polite, pained expressions of men about to perform an unpleasant duty. The board turned me down.

I was still smarting from the verdict when I got a call early the next morning from board member Uly Da Parma. He was one of the few who had liked my idea. But his first words didn't do anything to restore me to a sunny disposition.

"Hank," he said, "that thing yesterday was your fault."

"My fault?" I bristled.

"Your fault," he repeated firmly. "You just walked in there and sprang it cold. They were flabbergasted. You have to remember that you have lived with this all your life but for others it is still new. Next time, do a little spade work. Get your board members off one at a time and give them facts, figures, specific programs. Don't call for a decision until you know you've got the votes. I think you can swing this thing if you really try."

He was right as always. Once again I learned the lessons of persuasion and patience. I worked out all the details, logically, clearly, then lobbied like any legislator trying to get a pet measure through. I lined up a vote here, a vote there, got commitments of "I'll go along if the others don't object." And a few months later the board approved the idea by unanimous vote. Bassett announced the decision with a wry smile.

"All right, Hank, you've got your program. Now all you have to do is go get the money."

We called it Human Resources Corporation. It was set up as a nonprofit organization with separate funds and a separate staff. But before we could hire a staff, or even print a letterhead, a big teaching job fell in our laps.

It happened as a result of the talks I was forever giving to business and professional groups. A soft-spoken, mild looking man came up after one such talk and announced that he was interested. "I'd like to see your program put into practice in my company," he said.

"Good. What company?"

"Sears, Roebuck and Company."

That could be a tremendous break. But I wondered how much weight this man could swing.

"May I ask what your job is there?"

"I'm chairman of the board."

"Oh!" I blushed and recovered as best I could. "Then you don't have much to look forward to, do you?"

T. V. Houser—the Sears, Roebuck chairman— shortly demonstrated the qualities which made him the boss. In a matter of weeks, Sears, Roebuck was re-writing its employment manual, throwing out clauses which discriminated against the disabled. Suddenly a huge new opportunity opened up for the disabled at a firm which employs 250,000 people.

Houser arranged for his top aides to visit our plant and see what we were doing. By the time the plans were completed, the seminar was expanded to include repre-sentatives from a dozen industrial giants—General Electric, Remington Rand, S. H. Kress, U. S. Steel, Bulova Watch, duPont, U. S. Rubber, Metropolitan Life.

One of the high moments of the seminar was a simple walk through the aisles at our shop. The businessmen saw hard at work "misfits" and "unemployables" of every kind—amputees, epileptics, the deaf, dumb and blind, people twisted by bone defects, or shaking with palsy or frozen rigid by fusions.

An executive turned to me with tears in his eyes. "Now I know what you mean when you say 'nothing is impossible.'"

We stopped at a bench where a skilled workman demonstrated an intricate bit of electronic assembly. As we moved away, a member of the party nudged my elbow.

"Is everyone here disabled, Mr. Viscardi? What about that fellow we just talked to?"

"You couldn't spot it, eh? He lost both feet in a railroad accident. Of course, it's not really a disability here, because he doesn't work with his feet."

A conference followed the tour. There wasn't room in my office for the outsized group so we set up chairs in the yard, under the trees. Some children were playing ball in a fenced-off lot next door but we were too deep in discussion to be bothered by occasional raucous shouts. When a ball bounced over the fence, a Sears, Roebuck vice president scooped it up and tossed it expertly back while the meeting went on without a pause.

Art Nierenberg, Lou Blersch, Ronnie LeMieux and Frank Rieger gave short talks describing our methods, telling how they ran their departments. They made a striking impression—all in wheelchairs, all Abilities trained, all astonishingly young for the top management responsibilities they carried in a company already grossing more than half a million dollars a year. Art, at 27, was the oldest of the four. When they had finished, a personnel man from one of the big firms turned to me with an admiring comment.

"Where do you get men like these?"

"From your rejection lists," I said with a grin.

Several others made reports. We cited production and quality records which beat anything our competitors were doing. And a safety record of three years without a serious accident. But it was the personnel report that stole the show. Ellen Vaughan, our pert little personnel manager, was bombarded with questions.

Someone wanted to know what tests we applied to job applicants.

"I'm afraid we're not very scientific," Ellen said. "You see, people come here because they can't pass any of the so-called tests. Many of our workers were injured in childhood and left school at an early age. That knocks them out on education tests alone. About 90 per cent of them have never held another job. And almost all of them are physically disqualified by any ordinary standard. We disregard all that. We just talk to a prospect, try to size him up. If he really wants to work, we consider him qualified in the most important respect."

A visitor asked about time lost through sickness. Ellen delved into a file and extracted one of her well-kept records.

"I'll give you last year's report. Our employees averaged 1.2 days of sick leave per 100 working days, compared with 1.3 days at the usual shop. Absenteeism was only .8 days compared to the usual 3.3. There's no mystery about it, gentlemen. We come to work because we love our jobs. People show up here during snow-storms and hurricanes which close other plants for miles around."

Where did we draw the line at medical risk?

"That's a tough one," Ellen admitted. "We hire a man first, then have a doctor examine him. Sometimes the report comes back that he's unemployable and we answer: 'He can't be. He's already at work.' But it can be a hard decision to make."

Ellen produced another file. "Here's a case history. A man you probably met on your tour of the plant. He's 45 years old, has a bad heart, and a wife and three children to support. He lost his previous job after a heart attack and was unemployed for several years. He came to us and said that if he has to chance another attack he'd rather get it from work than from worry. We think he has the right to choose his risks. We know he needs the job."

Did we consider anyone unemployable?

"Yes, of course," Ellen conceded. "Last week, for instance, a young man applied here. He was about 30 years old, paralyzed from the waist down, and had lived with his parents all his life. His mother came with him and insisted on answering all the questions. I tried to ease her out of the interview, but she wouldn't let him go. And he was lost without her. He kept saying mother this, mother that, turning to her for every opinion. I had to reject him. He wasn't ready for Abilities. He hadn't grown up. The one who really wanted to work was the mother. We couldn't hire her."

A visitor thought that didn't quite answer the question. Surely there must be some who were unemployable for purely physical reasons. Did we have a standard on that?

"Yes," said Ellen, "we have a standard. Our rough rule of thumb is that we will consider anyone who can get to the plant by his own devices. We automatically reject anyone who wants us to furnish the transportation."

She looked around, saw that the point was not fully understood. "That's a much tougher 'examination' than you might suppose," Ellen continued. "Many of our people have to ride the buses at rush hour. They'll tell you that it's the hardest thing they do all day. And yet some of them come 25 miles or more, change buses three or four times, and do it twice a day every day in all kinds of weather. If they have strength enough and determination enough to do that, we feel that they are able to sit quietly at a bench and lace wires or work with light tools."

Sitting in her wheelchair, Ellen seemed serenely unaware that she herself was eloquent testimony of what the disabled could do. But no one else missed the point. The personnel man next to me was wholly swept away from the traditional caution of his calling.

"Your system makes sense," he declared. "It makes more sense than all the questionnaires and examinations."

We put our first teaching session down as a smashing success.

The Sears, Roebuck conference was the first of many. In one six-month period in 1956 we had 1200 visitors from 22 countries—businessmen, government representatives, physicians, psychologists, plant safety engineers, rehabilitation experts of every kind.

Viscardi in the same period got pretty weary of packing clean shirt and toilet kit to catch the next plane. I covered 12,000 miles, spoke to more than 15,000 people, addressed meetings as far away as Cuba. But the most important engagement was a short journey to speak before a small group of very powerful men.

The Senate Finance Committee was holding hearings in Washington on a bill which provided for social security retirement of disabled persons at age 50. I distrusted the measure; it seemed a first step toward a disabled solution of "pension them off." I was asked to appear and state my views.

It was not an easy question for me. I knew that the bill would provide immediate aid for disabled people who couldn't work, or couldn't get work. I feared, however, that in the long run it would do much more harm than good.

A business association got in touch with me. They wanted the measure defeated but not on my grounds. All they seemed to care about was the possibility of higher taxes. They offered to provide my transportation to Washington and take care of me while I was there.

"No, thanks," I said. "I will go on my own if I go at all."

I turned to Uly for advice but this time he couldn't help me.

"This is one of those lonely decisions you must make," he said. "It would be easy to tell you to stay home, stay out of it. But you must live with yourself. Which ever way you testify you will make enemies. Don't go and you may only have to deal with the enemies you already have."

I decided to go.

On the appointed day I found myself in a witness chair, facing six senators who looked down on me from the elevated eminence of a huge horseshoe desk. The hearing chamber was a great, high-ceilinged room, austere and impressive. For a moment I felt intimidated by the trappings with which official Washington conducts its business. Senator Byrd of Virginia put me at my ease with a few words of gracious welcome.

"I was born without limbs," I began, "and I have

spent my life close to this problem of disability. I have a great faith that solutions can be found in the competitive, free enterprise spirit of our country."

In brief outline I sketched for the senators what Abilities had achieved. I described how we had produced more than a million dollars worth of goods in the first three years, how we paid out more than $600,000 in salaries to people who were supposed to be hopelessly disabled. I stressed the fact that many of our workers were still leading active, useful lives at 60, 70, even 80.

I tried to express the enormous yearning which gave force and meaning to our effort:

"Our disabled people cry for the right to be the same as others. They want to be considered as the ordinary people they really are, each according to his individual capacities and abilities, each with his compensating qualities to offset the extremes of physical make-up.

"None of us is without limitations. But sheer physical strength is no measure of ability.

"Homer could have squatted in the dust at the gates of Athens. The rich would have pitied him and tossed gold into his cap because he, like Milton, was blind.

"Julius Caesar, the first general, statesman and historian of his age and, excepting Cicero, its greatest orator, a mathematician, a philologist, a jurist, an architect—he was an epileptic.

"There are no disabled people—only people. The extremes of physical suffering carry with it a great complement, the patience to struggle.

"There is nothing which can substitute for this basic human right; no honors, no pensions, no parades, no subsidy, can replace the wish to live and work in dignity, in free and open competition with all the world."

I had intended a crisp, factual statement but the floodgates of emotion had opened and the words had come rushing out. Now I caught hold of myself. "I regret that I have no recommendations to make; only grave apprehensions. Should we stigmatize our disabled people with a productive age limit of 50, we might seem to condone the ignorance and prejudice that now prevents them from exercising the abilities they have."

The presentation excited comment—and controversy. Several of the senators commended my stand; the chief clerk of the committee termed the testimony "the finest ever received during the thirteen years I have been on the committee staff."

Much of the press was in my corner, too. Wrote the *Christian Science Monitor:* "It was as though a fresh breeze of inspiration had suddenly swept the room clean of dusty, time-tangled convention. It would have indeed been difficult for anyone at that moment to define the term 'disability.'"

From some others came sharp and angry reactions. For weeks I received letters charging that I had struck a cruel blow at the hopes of people who desperately needed government aid.

The critics, many of them, were generous, well-meaning citizens who wanted to serve as their brothers' keepers. But as I pondered their letters I found myself wondering how they would like to be cast in the role of the kept.

Other letters were from disabled people who bitterly complained that I had let them down, sold them out. These were the hardest to answer.

Another journey was sentimental and purely personal. I went back to Fordham University, my old alma mater, to receive a much belated degree.

Fordham meant a great deal to me. It was the place where a young and eager Viscardi spent three of the happiest years of his life.

I ran my stumps to the bone there, trying to earn a few extra dollars as busboy, gym assistant, library clerk. And then sat up half the night more often than not, nursing a bottle of prohibition beer, participating in the sometimes lighthearted, sometimes terribly earnest talk of college bull sessions.

It was the place where I discovered the exciting, unlimited world of knowledge. I dreamed of becoming a lawyer, perhaps a priest.

It was the place, too, where I discovered the economic facts of life. The big depression was on. The Viscardis were poor. My odd jobs were not enough. In my junior year I had to leave because I was deep in debt.

Now I was back, donning a black robe and flat-topped

hat to receive an honorary LL.D. Fordham seemed unchanged and timeless; the Gothic towers were as graceful as ever and the Jesuit instructors might have stepped out of my memory book as they walked the campus with belted cassocks swaying stiffly. But I had changed a lot in 21 years. I tried in vain to recapture the warm sensations of another time. The whole experience seemed curiously unreal.

A flutter of white handkerchief caught my eye as I took my place in the procession line. Lucile was waiting along the processional path. Six-year-old Nina clasped her hand and looked very solemn; four-year-old Donna peeped out mischievously from behind her skirts. I saluted them with a grave wink when I passed and Donna responded with a glad shout of "Daddy!"

That took care of the unreal feeling. There was no doubting the reality of those three.

The columns reached the steps leading up to a platform. I took the arm of my sponsor, Father Charles J. Deane, a Jesuit patriarch for whom I had served many a mass in my undergraduate days. I flexed my aluminum legs, lifted one well-shod willow foot after the other, executed a neat left turn at the top of the steps.

The tough-minded old German craftsman who made my first legs had taught me how to take steps like these. A flash of recall brought back the way he used to drill me, shouting guttural cadence to marching music. Like the music which was swelling now.

A lot of others had helped me up the steps. Doc Yanover. Bernard Baruch. Eleanor Roosevelt. Preston Bassett. Uly Da Parma. And many, many more. I said a quick little prayer of thanks for all of them.

I was standing in front of the bishop, waiting to receive my degree. There was an unexpected lump in my throat but I covered up with a whispered wisecrack.

"Sorry, Your Excellency, I can't kneel. These must be atheist legs."

"My son," he said kindly, "I will kneel for you."

Somehow, despite too much time devoted to speeches and ceremonies, the business flourished and my tribe increased.

Lucile presented me with our fourth daughter—a bright-eyed, black-haired little charmer, as saucy as the mother and named after her.

Abilities grew like the seed that fell on fertile ground. By the end of our fifth year we had hired more than 330 people. Once again we overflowed from a jampacked shop and had to set up benches in the yard.

This time we wouldn't settle for a makeshift expansion. We were ready to build our own plant. We wanted the best.

Director Arthur Roth thought we should finance the building through a corporate bond issue. A board member asked who would guarantee the bonds.

"Why," said Roth, "I suppose we all will. I can't think of a sounder investment in America today."

From Roth, a conservative banker, that was high praise indeed.

There remained the question of where to put the building. Land was even higher than before. For weeks I chased leads, met with brokers. I couldn't find anything that came even close to our needs at our price.

After one frustrating session with a broker I was walking through the Garden City Hotel lobby when I was hailed by a familiar voice.

"Why the gloomy look, friend? Having trouble counting the money those so-called cripples are making?" It was Paul Townsend, an old friend whose public relations office was partly in the hotel's bar. "Have a drink with a poor working man," he suggested.

The drink sounded inviting. I found myself bending Paul's ear with my land troubles.

"I've got just the man for you," he said. "Ernie Blaich. He's head of the Roslyn Savings Bank, runs a pretty good real estate business in Manhasset besides. Let's talk to him. If there's a deal open anywhere, Ernie knows about it."

Blaich was a round, comfortable, kindly looking man; he had heard all about Abilities and seemed delighted that we were coming to him for help. "If there is land available in this area for speculation," he said, "there should be land for this worthwhile purpose. Have breakfast with me tomorrow at the bank. I'll have some of my associates prepare tentative sites and we can look over the maps."

The next morning over coffee and sweet rolls we selected three possible locations from the maps. Ernie and I took off to see them first hand.

We made the first stop at Albertson, Long Island, and I knew at once that I'd found what I was looking for. It was a big tract, convenient for every purpose, set down in the midst of quiet suburban homes. A pleasant little brook ran through the adjoining woods. I could visualize our people enjoying noon hour picnics under the trees. It was perfect.

Blaich told me that it was owned by Harold Gleason. "A hard man to bargain with," he told me. "But you work on him, and I'll work on him, and we'll see."

Gleason's asking price was $90,000. He wouldn't come to my office to discuss the deal, fearing perhaps that if he had a look at Abilities it might influence his business judgment. However, he wasn't nearly as flinty as he tried to make out. One day he phoned me.

"The price on that parcel has gone up," he announced.

"Gone up?"

"Yes, I'm asking $100,000 now. However, I have decided to donate a $60,000 piece of the property to your Human Resources Corporation. The other $40,000 is cash to Abilities."

"Mr. Gleason, this is very generous. . . . "

He cut me off brusquely. "Don't thank me. Thank those bandits who write the tax laws. The government would get it if I didn't give it to you. It works out that I'll make about as much as I'm able to keep."

This time I didn't hesitate to accept a contribution. Partly that reflected the fact that the new plant would be used by both Abilities and Human Resources. Partly it reflected my confidence in our growing success. Abilities was so solidly established that I no longer felt the least fear for our independence.

In fact, I went beyond just accepting the contribution. I asked for an extra concession.

"Mr. Gleason," I said, "would you consider extending our payment to two installments beyond the calendar year? The tax advantage might be even greater for you."

"That sounds all right," he said thoughtfully. "Say, I was told you were the dedicated type, one of those impractical fellows. The way you do business, maybe you should come and work for me."

"No, thanks," I told him. "I'm going to be pretty busy trying to raise the first installment of $20,000."

There was a twinkle in Ernie's eye when I reported to him on mission completed.

We were all set. Or almost all set. Then a phone call warned that there was still a battle to be fought.

"I've received a circular," the caller said, "which informs me that you're bringing a factory into our community. It says your trucks will clog our streets and endanger our children. It claims that home values will be destroyed by smoke and noise. A protest meeting is being held at the Albertson Fire House tonight."

"Who are you?" I asked. "Why are you calling me?"

"I'm a schoolteacher. I've found that there are usually two sides to a story and I'd like to hear yours."

"You will," I promised. "I didn't know about the meeting but I'll make it a point to be there."

He hesitated. "I don't have any authority to invite you. You could just barge in, I suppose, but I'm afraid you'll find some folks pretty antagonistic."

"That's all right," I assured him. "I don't mind a good scrap. And thanks a lot for letting me know."

I put in a quick call to Uly for advice. I knew his company had faced the same problem when moving branches into suburban communities.

"If the majority of the community doesn't want you, go elsewhere," Uly said. "But don't be frightened off by an organized minority. And remember, be tactful. You can't afford to get mad."

There was just time that evening to make the meeting. I gobbled a drugstore sandwich, giving regretful thought to the fine dinner that was waiting at home, and headed for Albertson. Some two hundred irate citizens had already assembled at the Fire House by the time I arrived.

It wasn't a meeting so much as a pep rally for people who had already made up their minds. They were convinced that Abilities would be an eyesore, a hazard, a drag on home values. From some of the speakers came an ugly undercurrent, a thinly disguised complaint that "those cripples" would lower the tone of the neighborhood.

Viscardi talked long and hard. I showed them artist's sketches of our new building, as sleek and handsome as a modern school. I told them of the research and training phases of our program. A few in the audience seemed to be moved, but the others were hopeless. They weren't interested in facts which contradicted their fears.

"Don't listen to his fancy talk," shouted a man from the rear of the hall. "Let him call it by another name but a factory is a factory. That's what he wants to build."

Don't get mad, Uly had said. But I got mad.

"You people can take any action you like," I told them, "but you're not going to run us out. I don't believe that you represent a fraction of one per cent of community sentiment."

They took a vote then to demonstrate solidarity and it came out something like 199 to 1 against us. My new friend, the school teacher, was the lonely holdout in the crowd.

It was past midnight when I got home, worn out from the long day and sick with frustration and anger. Lucile took one look at my face and knew how it had gone. She eased me into the most comfortable chair and thrust a warm cup of tea into my hand.

"Bad, huh?"

"Terrible. They wouldn't even listen. They're out to block us in every way they can."

"So they're out to block us." Lucile perched on the arm of my chair, shook her pretty head in mock dismay. "That's too bad for them, isn't it? They don't know what they're taking on."

The second round of the battle was fought at a zoning board hearing. The board chairman was a local real estate man, a thin, wiry fellow dressed in slacks, sleeveless sweater and camel's hair jacket. A beret lay at his elbow. I eyed him apprehensively. A country gardener type, I thought. Quite possibly one of those genteel people who want to fence off their communities and shut out the real world. But he listened courteously to our arguments. He inspected with interest our architect's sketch of the proposed building. Perhaps we were wanted, after all. I didn't know whether to feel relieved or worried when he adjourned the hearing without immediate decision.

I expected a dawdling deliberation, but twenty-four hours later the verdict was in. The zoning board approved our application. A jubilant Viscardi vowed that he would never again form snap judgments about men who attended meetings bedecked in berets.

But that didn't end it. The opposition girded for Round Three. They thought we had to go to the local Town Board for final approval and they were prepared to make it a hot political issue. They didn't know we had dug up a legal finding which allowed us to proceed without further hearings unless an appeal was filed within ninety days.

For weeks they staged meetings, trying to discourage me and wear me down. I attended every meeting, seeming to be patient and hesitant, anxious to settle the last argument before making a move. Over and over I assured them that we did light, clean work which would not disturb the community in any way. Our architect's drawings became dog-eared and dirty from being passed around for endless inspection. I cited again and again the wealth our wage earners would bring to the town, the property taxes the plant would pay.

We began to win converts. The opposition dwindled to a hundred people, then to a hard core of fifty.

We also won time. Their lawyer still hadn't discovered what our lawyer had known from the first. The ninety days came and went and the die-hards did not file an appeal.

On the ninety-first day I answered a telephone and heard again the all-too-familiar voice of the group's leader.

"We're scheduling another meeting on that factory matter. I suppose you'll want to attend as usual?"

"No," I said, "I don't think so. I think I'll just go ahead and build the plant."

"You can't do that!"

"The hell I can't. I would suggest, sir, that you read the law."

There was a satisfying click when I hung up.

A sleek, up-to-date $650,000 building was rising on the property. It was as solid as the brick walls that enclosed it, as airy as the huge picture windows that afforded sweeping views of the wooded countryside. And it was tailor-made for us. Wide, gently sloping ramps provided easy passage for those who walked with difficulty, or not at all. The doors had special latches instead of knobs so that those who used hooks for hands would not have to fumble. Even the water coolers were specially designed, with extra outlets for those at wheelchair level.

There were large private offices for the supervisors, recreation areas for the employees, a fine cafeteria, a conference room, a whole wing of shiny new medical rooms which would excite the envy of many a hospital.

Tucked away in one corner of the building was a chapel designed with eloquent simplicity. Three altars were provided—one each for the Protestant, the Jewish and my own Catholic faith.

The chapel would provide a service for Abilities people who found it difficult or impossible to attend church or synagogue because of crowds, high stairs and other obstacles. More than that, it expressed the deep spiritual urge behind our efforts. To me at least Abilities signified worship of God through service to man. It was almost my living prayer.

Along with all these special features was 40,000 square feet of wonderful floor space in which to work. Soon the floors would be studded with machines and equipment, designed like the shop itself, for our people and their needs.

A lot of love and labor had gone into that building. A lot of hope and fear and sweat and struggle. It was a monument to every man and woman who worked in our shop.

It meant most to the oldtimers, the ones who had come up with us from grimy beginnings in an unfurnished garage. For one of those oldtimers, Dinah Craik, I reserved a special premiere.

Dinah had been our first woman employee, one of our first blind people. Number 13 on the payroll. She was the one who added that ingenious woman's touch to our early harness lacing routine—the bobby pins which kept the wires from slipping as they were laced together.

She had worked hard and well in almost every department and had received in turn something more than a job. With Abilities help and encouragement, she had undergone the corneal transplants which were at that time a new miracle of medical skill.

Corneas are the thin, clear windowpanes of the eye. Doctors take them from dead people who have passed on parts of their bodies to others as a last thoughtful bequest. Carefully, very carefully, because one cornea can provide windows for many blind eyes, the doctors cut the material into tiny segments. Then the glasslike segments are sewn very precisely over the pupils of afflicted eyes. Such was Dinah's operation. It was not a guaranteed miracle by any means—sometimes it works and sometimes not—but it offered hope where there was none before.

Dinah's operation hung for days in an anguished balance between success and failure. Forces which science only half understands contended for the life or death of the tissues transplanted into her body. She saw brilliant, tantalizing flashes of light. Then darkness enclosed her again. The operation had failed.

Dinah took it as she did everything else, without a whisper of complaint. When the opportunity came to try again she was ready to endure again the agonizing uncertainty.

This time the operation worked. Not perfectly, but much better than before. She was able to make out the large letters on an eye chart. She threw away her white cane. She saw her husband's face for the first time in fifteen years. She could distinguish by sight alone between her two grandchildren, knew even the shades of difference in the color of their hair. The vision might or might not fade again but for a little while at least she was able to see those whom she cherished most.

There was something else I wanted Dinah to see. One afternoon I stopped by her bench.

"How about my driving you home tomorrow night? Tell your daughter not to bother picking you up."

When she climbed into my car the next evening I suggested a drive and she agreed. I didn't tell her where we were going but I think she knew. We rode along relaxed and quiet, a couple of old comrades who didn't need to fill in the passing moments with empty chatter. We turned off at Albertson and I pulled up at the plant site.

"Well, there it is, Dinah. The new home of Abilities, Inc."

We got out of the car and walked up the circular drive and stood on the bridge over the little winding brook. The trees around us were green with the promise of spring. A little distance away was the new building where workmen even now were pouring concrete for the terrace.

"The terrace is where we'll eat lunch in fine weather," I said. "Just inside is the cafeteria. We can use that for a recreation room, too. And down there, beside the brook, is where we'll set up the tables for plant picnics."

We leaned on the bridge railing and stood looking

for many minutes at what we had built. Finally Dinah turned to me with those still half-blind eyes, the eyes which could see everything because her heart was receptive. She broke the long silence.

"It's beautiful, Hank. It's just beautiful."

where else. I'm thinking particularly of the crippled kids."

Art's eyes were shining at the prospect. I leaned forward and tapped the blueprint.

"Look here," I said. "Here's the swimming pool you always wanted for hydrotherapy."

"Gosh, Hank, do you think the directors will go for that?"

"Of course they won't. Not at first. But we'll work on them, Art. We'll work on them. They'll come around."

Art folded the plans carefully, laid them back on my desk. "It's a nice dream." He turned to me, suddenly very serious. "Hank, what do you really think? Where will this thing end? How far can we go?"

"Who can say? Some of the big companies, the real giants, started as we did with a few men bent over benches and desks. We could be a giant some day.

"Don't forget, Art, that we have a big advantage, something special going for us. We have friends—in business, in labor, in government, in every walk of life. We're not alone. We've never been alone.

"Maybe," I added musingly, "we'll succeed so well some day that we'll work ourselves out of business. If the day comes when a disabled man or woman can walk into any plant in America, and get a job, then Abilities can mark mission completed and close its doors."

Nierenberg cocked a skeptical eyebrow and I nodded agreement with what he was thinking.

"Yes, I know. That's looking a long, long way down the road. Perhaps the next generation will see it."

So ends the Abilities story. With memories still fresh of yesterday's struggle and hardship and with the bright promise of tomorrow's hopes and dreams.

In truth, however, there is no end. No end to dreams, certainly. No end to struggle either so long as dreams exceed reality.

The real end lies hidden in some distant future. But of some things we are very sure.

We will go on growing and changing because to cease growth and change is the beginning of death. And we are enormously alive.

We understand the dangers of climbing to new heights. We may slip and fall back and have to hold on again for dear life. That prospect does not terrify us. We are good at holding on.

At some point no doubt we will know another time of adversity. When it comes, we will grapple with it as we have grappled with our own disordered bodies, and we will win. We know how to win. We have learned in a hard school an essential rule of human existence.

We expect to struggle for the rest of our lives. All we ask is the right to struggle.

+1+

114

E.R.
127 - E.R.
135